ANCIENT WISDOM

STOIC LESSONS *for* SELF-MASTERY

MIKE ETTORE
U.S. MARINE CORPS (RETIRED)

Fidelis Leadership Group
— Developing World Class Leaders —

Ancient Wisdom:
Stoic Lessons for Self-Mastery

Paperback ISBN: 978-1-7372881-3-8
Hardcover ISBN: 978-1-7372881-2-1
Ebook ISBN: 978-1-7372881-4-5

This book is dedicated to my children,

Michelle, Larry, Mike II, and Majda,

in appreciation for their unwavering love, kindness, patience, and support. Throughout their lives, depending on the situation at hand, they have been exposed to various versions of me, ranging from a calm and serene Seneca-like mentor, advisor, and guide, to a firebreathing hybrid of Genghis Khan, Teddy Roosevelt, and Marine Corps father à la "The Great Santini," who encouraged them to "dominate the battlefield," "take no prisoners," and to "rip the lungs out" of anyone or anything posing a threat to them. I want them to know how much I love them, and I hope by reading this book, they will gain further insight into what goes on in the mind of the "Old Man," and why, for better or for worse, he is who he is!

Contents

About the Cover

This ancient frieze is named Conquest and Clemency and was originally placed on the Arch of Marcus Aurelius, which was created in 165 A.D. in Libya.

Thanks to a four-line inscription on the arch, we know it was built in honor of Emperor Marcus Aurelius and Lucius Verus, who was the adoptive brother of Marcus Aurelius.

The triumphal arch was erected in large part to commemorate recent victories over the Parthians. Dressed in a cuirass, Marcus Aurelius appears on horseback as he surveys the battlefield. At his feet are defeated barbarians begging for mercy.

The frieze was removed from the arch and is now displayed in the Capitoline Museum in Rome, Italy.

Introduction

Frederick the Great, George Washington, Theodore Roosevelt, and many of today's most notable leaders, intellectuals, and high achievers learned to embrace the wisdom of the ancient Stoics as they sought to live happy, successful, and productive lives.

This book uniquely combines insights from Marcus Aurelius, Seneca, Epictetus and other Stoic philosophers with the author's interpretations, musings, and life-time of experiences and lessons learned. The result is an easy-to-read book containing timeless wisdom and empowering advice that can help readers learn how to dramatically alter and control their emotional responses to life's inevitable challenges and obstacles.

Orientation to Stoicism

"Of all people, only those are at leisure who make time for philosophy, only they truly live. Not satisfied to merely keep good watch over their days, they annex every age to their own. All the harvest of the past is added to their store."

—SENECA

I have, even from a very young age, sought to become the best person I could possibly be. As I endeavored to accomplish that goal, I realized that there is great value in reflecting upon the experiences, insights, and advice of others. Soon after I enlisted in the U.S. Marine Corps in 1974, I realized that I was surrounded by some incredibly wise men, many who had fought in World War II, Korea, and Vietnam, and had gained superb insights through their experiences on the battlefield. I was greatly impressed by these men and their humility, selflessness, self-confidence, and willingness to help anyone who sought their wise counsel.

I was able to learn, via interaction with older, more seasoned Marines, that most of them were avid students of history. Their quest for knowledge was focused on any lessons that would help one become a better person, leader, and warrior. Seeing that some of the very best of these leaders were active students of various ancient philosophers, I began to read and learn more about these old, wise men who had lived many hundreds or even thousands of years before I was born. This resulted in my introduction to Stoicism, and I developed an instant affinity for everything associated with this ancient philosophy of life.

Reading the lessons and advice of ancient teachers who lived remarkable lives based on certain fundamental principles and virtues led to my resolve to make every effort to model my life after the time-tested values, precepts, and instructions that they lived by and taught.

The philosophy and lessons of Stoicism have been drawn from the private notes and diaries of Marcus Aurelius, who was one of Rome's most extraordinary emperors; the teachings of Seneca, a playwright and a wise man; and the documents of Epictetus, a slave who later became a very influential teacher. These men laid the foundation for what we now refer to as Stoicism—the guiding principles for the civic disciplines in much of the developing western world and practiced by anyone in the pursuit of living the Good Life, irrespective of class, status, or background.

I've found that Stoicism, as a concept in modern times, is often grossly misunderstood and viewed as a philosophy of life devoid of emotion. To the untutored, it can appear to be a rather boring and bland approach to life. I understand this skepticism well, because as a new student of Stoicism, I too assumed that this way of life was associated with overly harsh and demanding requirements of people who were simply looking for a path to follow that could help them become better people and assist them in accomplishing their dreams and goals.

Upon studying and digging deeper into the tenets of Stoicism, I discovered that it is a *tool* that could help anyone who was in the pursuit of self-mastery, wisdom, courage, and perseverance. I also discovered that some of the greatest leaders and influencers of the past were students of Stoicism, including Frederick the Great, George Washington, Eugène Delacroix, Adam Smith, Immanuel Kant, Thomas Jefferson, Theodore Roosevelt, William Alexander Percy, Ralph Waldo Emerson, Walt Whitman, Beatrice Webb, Matthew Arnold, J.K. Rowling, and Ambrose Bierce.

Stoicism can be summarized as a simple guide for living a righteous life, which then leads to a prosperous, productive, and rewarding one. In the following paragraphs you'll find a very quick history of how stoicism came to be and the pillars upon which it is rooted.

The Origin of Stoicism

The origins of Stoicism can be attributed to a merchant named Zeno, around the year 304 BC, after a shipwreck while he was traveling to Athens. It was at this time that he was introduced to philosophy after meeting the Cynic Philosopher Crates and the Magarian philosopher, Stilpo. He had remarked, "I made a prosperous voyage when I suffered shipwreck." Zeno and his disciples would often meet at the *stoa poikile* (meaning "painted porch," erected in the 5th century BC). At this place, the insights and lessons that would later become the foundation of Stoicism were discussed and developed.

The Four Virtues Of Stoicism

Stoicism strives to elevate the lives of men to the highest good. This was referred to as *Summum Bonum*, an expression coined by Cicero, a Roman Orator. As a young man trying to figure things out, I remember asking myself a few questions: what is the purpose of living? What am I aiming for in life, and how do I get there? By delving into the philosophy of the stoics, I realized what the aim was: Virtue—living a good or virtuous life.

In Stoicism, there are four fundamental virtues that are regarded as the driving force behind all that a person does in life: Courage, Temperance, Justice, and Wisdom, and by following these four basic virtues, all else will fall into place: happiness, reputation, wealth, fame, love, and honor.

I believe these virtues are timeless and are as relevant today as they were many centuries ago. Despite the incredible advancements in technology and other aspects of modern life, we can't still find a substitute for being brave, maintaining moderation and sobriety, standing for truth, and doing the right thing.

"The man who has virtue is in need of nothing whatever for the purpose of living well."

—Cicero

1. Courage

Stoicism teaches that courage is possessing the mental or moral strength to persevere and withstand fear, difficulty, or danger. It is an essential virtue for surviving in life. Seneca wrote: "you have passed through life without an opponent. No one can ever know what you are capable of, not even you."

It was Epictetus who mentioned that every man should commit two words to heart: Persist and resist.

Courage demands that we go through life undaunted and unintimidated by the problems that come our way, and to see our trials and tribulations as opportunities to build character. Courage helps us hold onto our core values and guiding principles. Courage ensures we insist on the truth regardless of the consequences.

"Don't you know life is like a military campaign? One must serve on watch, another in reconnaissance, another on the front line. . . . So it is for us—each person's life is a kind of battle, and a long and varied one too. You must keep watch like a soldier and do everything commanded. . . . You have been stationed in a key post, not some lowly place, and not for a short time but for life."

—EPICTETUS, *DISCOURSES*

2. *Temperance*

As I matured, I came to understand that while courage is important, I had to remain vigilant that it didn't cause me to act recklessly and end up putting myself or my loved ones, my fellow Marines, and later on, business colleagues in danger or harm's way. Aristotle had called this vigilance and balanced approach to courage the *Golden Mean*, which is the appropriate amount of courage needed for any situation—not too small and not too much—just the right amount. It is in this aspect that the virtue of temperance plays a critical role in Stoicism.

Temperance is the virtue of doing nothing in excess. It is doing the right thing, in the right amount in the right way. Aristotle had also mentioned that "we are what we repeatedly do, therefore excellence is not an act, but a habit." Epictetus said, "Curb your desire—don't set your heart on so many things and you will get what you need." And Seneca said, "You ask what is the proper limit to a person's wealth? First, having what is essential, and second, having what is enough."

The words of these wise men show that contentment and temperance go hand in hand. It is in this moderation that the balance needed to maintain an excellent life is found. Also, an excellent way of life and living is one that is built by observing and following certain habits, which compounds over time to form the desired character.

> *"If you seek tranquility, do less. Or (more accurately) do what's essential—what the logos of a social being requires, and in the requisite way. Which brings a double satisfaction: to do less, better. Because most of what we say and do is not essential. If you can eliminate it, you'll have more time and more tranquility. Ask yourself at every moment, 'Is this necessary?'"*
>
> **—MARCUS AURELIUS, *MEDITATIONS***

3. Justice

Justice is a paramount stoic virtue. It influences the other virtues. Marcus Aurelius had referred to Justice as the source of all other virtues. Throughout history, courageous men and women have risked or even sacrificed their personal freedom in order to ensure that Justice prevailed and willingly faced persecution, trials, and suffering in the course of defending the people and the ideas they loved.

Stoicism proposes that the man see the world clearly and try to make it a better place for every other human being to live happily. Through the virtue of justice, the stoics try to overcome evil and wrongdoings with good deeds and actions.

> *"And a commitment to Justice in your own acts. Which means: thought and action resulting in the common good. What you were born to do."*
>
> **—MARCUS AURELIUS, *MEDITATIONS***

4. Wisdom

Stoicism views wisdom as an essential virtue that must be present in anyone seeking to live the Good Life. Zeno said that we were given two ears and one mouth for a reason: to listen more and talk less. We also have two eyes which means we should also read and observe more than we talk.

In Diogenes Laërtius' Lives of the Eminent Philosophers, he wrote of the Stoics, "wisdom they define as the knowledge of things good and evil and of what is neither good nor evil . . . knowledge of what we ought to choose, what we ought to beware of, and what is indifferent."

I have discovered that wisdom is not just great amounts of information. We must be able to distinguish truth from falsehood, honesty from fraud, good sources from misguiding ones. It is vital to maintain an open mind; to be constantly willing to learn new things and try new ways of thinking. It is also vital we learn to filter true meaning from the many noises in our environment. Despite the noise in the form of information all around us, we must be able to take out the key and principal information, the correct knowledge required to give our lives meaning.

In conclusion, Stoicism understands that life is unpredictable, and while we often cannot control circumstances, we can surely control our thoughts and actions relative to anything that life brings our way.

I will conclude this chapter with this quote from Meditations:

"If at some point in your life, you should come across anything better than Justice, prudence, self-control, Courage—than a mind satisfied that it has succeeded in enabling you to act rationally, and satisfied to accept what's beyond its control—if you find

*anything better than that, embrace it without reservations—it must
be an extraordinary thing indeed—and enjoy it to the full.*

*But if nothing presents itself that's superior to the spirit that
lives within—the one that has subordinated individual desires
to itself, that discriminates among impressions, that has
broken free of physical temptations, and subordinated itself to
the gods, and looks out for human beings' welfare—if you find
that there's nothing more important or valuable than that, then
don't make room for anything but it."*

—Marcus Aurelius

Stoicism Lessons

Despite having been around for more than 2000 years, the lessons and insights of Stoicism are still relevant in this time and age. The time-tested Stoic virtues of courage, temperance, wisdom, and justice have aided many in their pursuit of a rewarding, productive life.

During my journey along the path of Stoicism, I have learned many valuable lessons that have had a profound impact upon every aspect of my professional life. Reflecting upon the experiences, insights, and advice of the ancient Stoic philosophers has unquestionably helped me become a more effective warrior, leader of and mentor to the Marines I was entrusted with, and also helped me successfully navigate the business battlefield of Corporate America while serving as a C-level executive.

On a more personal level, my study of Stoicism has surely helped me become a better parent, life partner, friend, and colleague. Whenever I found myself struggling with life's never-ending challenges and stressors, I inevitably found relevant wisdom and guidance in the words of the ancients. Simply put, I've never encountered a dilemma, challenge, or form of stress or anxiety that was not included in the discussions and teachings of these wise men.

Over the years, I began to formulate a list of Stoicism's major lessons as they applied to my life. I use this list as a form of high-level orientation and guidance for anyone that I am privileged to teach, coach, and mentor—I'd like to share them with you:

The Lessons of Stoicism

1. *Don't be afraid of death—use it to give your life value.*

Everyone will die, it is our eventual, inevitable destiny. The Stoics understood this and spent time meditating on death.

Work, daily activities, business responsibilities are a constant in our day-to-day lives; very little time is left for us to ponder our own death or the death of a loved one. The stoic philosophers often meditated on their mortality—*memento mori*, a Latin phrase meaning "remember that you [have to] die" was somewhat of a constant warning even during times of joy and triumph.

Although it may seem morbid or depressing to focus on death, the idea was that this practice liberated them from the fear of death, and thus freed them to truly embrace each moment. Meditating on death provides a means to transcend the fear of the inevitable and focus on things we can control—the things we can improve within ourselves.

Being aware that we can die at any moment will typically result in our determination to be a source of positivity in the world, and to develop a sense of urgency not to waste any time but instead make every moment count. The Romans called this *Carpe Diem:* to seize each day and live it out to the fullest.

"As each day arises, welcome it as the very best day of all, and make it your own possession. We must seize what flees."

—SENECA

2. Always see the bigger picture.

For as long as we walk on the surface of the earth, there will always exist problems and challenges. We can neither run away from them, nor avoid them. Marcus Aurelius used to teach that "Taking the view from above" or "Plato's view" would serve to give insight and perspective when facing difficulties.

Using this technique has helped me to walk through very difficult situations and overcome very daring challenges. Aurelius' teaching reminds us that in the face of any situation, our problems are insignificant in the grand scheme of things. As such, we should learn not to exaggerate their impact or severity.

The real value in this lesson is that it enables us to step back, assess the situation, adjust our view or perspective, and redirect our efforts and attitude as we respond to the challenge.

"Think of the whole universe of matter and how small your share."

—MARCUS AURELIUS

3. Don't worry about the things you can't change. Focus on what you can change.

It is indisputable that there are many aspects of our lives that we cannot change and have no control over. We've all been in situations when we wished we could stop something from happening or wished we could reverse something that has happened.

13

Although this aspect of life could be distressing, a vital lesson I learned from Stoicism is that despite the problem or condition we are in, there is only one thing we have control over, and that is how we react or respond to those problems or situations. I learned to focus on what I could change and strived to expand my circle of influence.

Stoicism taught me how to differentiate situations under my control and those that are not.

> *"The chief task in life is simply this: to identify and separate matters so that I can say clearly to myself which are externals not under my control, and which have to do with the choices I actually control."*
>
> **—EPICTETUS**

4. *Don't be surprised when bad things happen, be Prepared.*

I learned early in life that being proactive is much more preferable to having to be reactive. Although at the time I thought I was having irrational fears and being unnecessarily pessimistic, as I studied the lives and teachings of stoic philosophers, I learned that it was indeed the right thing to do in any given situation.

Understanding that things can go wrong shouldn't deter us from acting or taking the initiative; it is crucial to consider all the factors that may cause a venture to go wrong or even fail. This helps you prepare yourself on how to respond if and when it eventually happens.

The stoic philosophers I read about practiced *Premeditatio Malorum* ("the pre-meditation of evils") which meant foreseeing all that could go wrong in any situation and devising a response to each eventuality accordingly.

Although this mentality may seem counterintuitive—rather than focusing on the good; thinking positive thoughts—it's really all about balance. Life is not just made up of positives, but also of what we perceive as negatives—the misfortunes, tragedies, problems. Having a Pollyannaish view of life can only result in being unprepared for the realities of life. The prudent way to go through life is to be prepared for the unexpected and unforeseen. If not, when a setback or a misfortune eventually strikes us, it could have a severely negative impact on our will and spirit.

> *"To bear trials with a calm mind robs misfortune*
> *of its strength and burden."*
>
> **—SENECA**

The genuine positivity here comes from our response in the face of adversity.

5. *See every problem as an opportunity.*

Because challenges and adversity are inevitable in life, I came to the realization that I needed to equip myself with the tools to face them and conquer them. I learned to become comfortable in the discomfort of challenges and problems. This was a fundamental concept proposed by Friedrich Nietzsche, which he referred to as *amor fati,* which means love of fate.

It is crucial to understand that simply *accepting* what life throws at you is not enough. We must *embrace* the difficulties life presents to us. It is through the strife in life that we become stronger, more prepared . . . better!

We can quickly turn obstacles and situations into opportunities to build character and improve our personality. Embracing life's problems becomes a way to advance and improve.

*"The impediment to action advances action.
What stands in the way becomes the way."*

—MARCUS AURELIUS

6. There is no shame in asking for help.

As a man, I was raised to be independent. Like many other men, I would rather drown than ask for help. I believed that I could eventually figure things out on my own no matter how long it took. There was no reason to ask another person to help, no need to inconvenience another with my problems. Asking for help would injure my ego and take away my pride.

Although resilience is a worthy virtue every human should have, knowing when to ask for help is possibly an even more important trait we should all acquire in life. We do not exist in isolation and in order to more effectively coexist, we must learn to be interdependent. Marcus Aurelius knew when to ask for help and when to create an alliance that would guarantee the protection and prosperity of his empire. He knew the importance of being vulnerable and being willing to accept other people's help.

*"Don't be ashamed of needing help. You have a duty to fulfil
just like a soldier on the wall of battle. So what if you are
injured and can't climb up without another soldier's help?"*

—MARCUS AURELIUS

7. Always Be Contented

Contentment is a form of gratitude. Learning to appreciate what we have, finding its value and worth, and enjoying it is a step in the direction to attaining life's fulfillment and joy.

Especially with today's focus on materialistic desires, it is crucial to avoid being tempted by the constant endeavor to acquire possessions—in the end it is all simply stuff and cannot give you the fulfillment that you seek. This is a trait that we as parents should strive to cultivate and nourish in our children from infancy, through childhood, and then in the teenage years—we should give them everything they *need*, but should never give them everything they *want*.

> "He is a wise man who does not grieve for the things which he has not, but rejoices for those which he has."
>
> **—EPICTETUS**

8. Never Stop Learning.

As a child I had a natural curiosity that led me to constantly seek knowledge and answers to my many questions. As I matured and grew older and wiser, I developed the patience that is necessary for the learning process.

The more we know, the more we discover how much we don't know. Knowledge is limitless, and it requires humility to keep learning even after attaining some level of success, and patience to keep learning even after we have achieved specific goals.

People change, situations evolve, and life continually takes new forms, so one must remain flexible and maintain an open mind in order to keep on learning and improving.

It is important that you approach life with curiosity and understand that every person you encounter has some knowledge that you don't have and can teach you something you do not know.

Plato said many years ago: "the more I know, the more I realize I know nothing." The stoic philosophers were learners who never stopped seeking knowledge and truth. This awareness that there is always something more one can learn as well as an open desire to continuously seek knowledge prevents us from becoming arrogant and proud.

"As long as you live, keep learning how to live."

—SENECA

The Rolex Moment

This chapter is from my book titled, *Trust-Based Leadership™: Marine Corps Leadership Concepts for Today's Business Leaders.* I have included it to illustrate a dire situation in my life where I instinctively followed the fundamental precept of Stoicism, as described below:

> *"The chief task in life is simply this: to identify and separate matters so that I can say clearly to myself which are externals not under my control, and which have to do with the choices I actually control. Where then do I look for good and evil? Not to uncontrollable externals, but within myself to the choices that are my own . . . "*

> **—EPICTETUS**

I want to emphasize that I did nothing heroic during the long, dark, and dangerous night of February 6, 1984. Fortunately, and even though I wasn't consciously thinking about Stoicism at the time, I was able to act in alignment with the guidance of Epictetus, as I collected my thoughts, determined what was under my control and what wasn't, and made decisions and took actions that could have a positive impact upon the dilemma that my Marines and I were facing.

Chapter 70:
The Rolex Moment

When I was a young, enlisted Marine, I used to see many of my officers wearing Rolex dive watches. I loved the look of them in the same way that some people favor a certain model of car or boat. I would sometimes ask my lieutenants to let me hold their watches so I could get a closer look at them. One of them once let me wear his watch for a day when I was a DI; I was "profiling" around the area that day, for sure! I promised myself that if I ever achieved my goal of becoming a commissioned officer, I'd buy one as a reward.

In 1982, shortly after becoming an officer, I bought a Rolex Submariner from the PX catalog for $550; the list price was $1,150. My take home pay in 1982 was $425 every two weeks as a prior-enlisted second lieutenant, so this was a significant purchase. I wasn't married at the time, had no mortgage or other debt, and I knew that I'd probably never again be able to justify spending that kind of money on a watch.

My First "Rolex Moment"
During my Marine career, there were several occasions in which I looked at my watch late at night, noting the time and thinking—or in this example, being convinced—that I may not be alive in the morning.

The first time this happened, my Marines and I were located in a very dangerous area of West Beirut in Lebanon. The Lebanese Civil War was one conducted largely on religious grounds. It essentially pitted Muslims against Christians, as each group and a multitude of sub-groups, militias, etc., jockeyed for power and control. Generally speaking, the city of Beirut was divided into two halves. East Beirut (Christian) and West Beirut (Muslim).

In April of 1983, the US Embassy was destroyed by a suicide bomber who drove a delivery van packed with explosives up to the building's front doors and detonated a huge, improvised bomb the van was carrying. Sixty-three people were killed and many more were seriously injured. The embassy building itself was rendered unusable and operations were relocated to a group of buildings a short distance away, with the most sensitive embassy functions being conducted inside the British embassy.

Upon arriving in Lebanon in early November after participating in operations in Grenada, I (along with my superb platoon sergeant, Staff Sergeant Mike Marshall) was tasked with leading my rein-forced rifle platoon as it guarded the large area in which the various "embassy buildings" were located. My beefed-up platoon now con-sisted of 104 Marines, most of whom were infantrymen, along with several extra communicators, a cook, extra Navy Corpsmen, and an amphibious tractor platoon led by Staff Sergeant Allan Chase.

That Night

The situation in Beirut had become incredibly volatile and dangerous in early February 1984. The violence had reached a level that many lifelong residents of the city had never previously experienced. These people had become almost desensitized to the violence associated with years of civil war but during this period of time, they realized that things had become worse than ever before.

On February 6, 1984, a battle between rival forces occupying East and West Beirut began. Each side began lobbing artillery and mortar rounds into their opponent's sector. And they did this with a fury that I will never forget.

During the evening, the area we were located in was getting pounded by artillery and mortar fire. The sound of small arms fire was non-stop and red and green tracer rounds were zipping through the air in all directions. The larger artillery rounds started getting closer to our positions and we could hear them whistling in prior to impacting as close as 50 meters from us on all sides of our perimeter. To use the proper tactical terminology to describe our plight, our defensive positions were now *bracketed* by the incoming artillery rounds; the more experienced Marines recognized this and knew that it was only a matter of time before the high-explosive projectiles started impacting directly on our positions.

To further complicate the tactical situation, radio contact with the battalion headquarters element located about five miles away was lost. I could not inform my chain of command of the situation, and while my senior leaders were aware that the entire city was in turmoil, they were not aware of the predicament that my Marines and I were facing.

After my leaders and I had done everything we could do from a tactical standpoint, it was simply time for us to hunker down and hope that we wouldn't get hit by any of the incoming shelling. Marines are taught that "hope is not a battlefield strategy" but, at this moment, it really was all that we had going for us.

At one point, an artillery round hit the building that some of my Marines and I were on top of. The round impacted about 20 feet below our rooftop position. The entire building shook and suffice it to say that amongst the Marines on that rooftop, the "pucker factor" was very high—probably the highest it had ever been for each of us. We were very lucky; just a tad higher and that round would have killed us all.

The artillery and mortar fire seemed to be increasing in volume and I assumed it would continue for another several hours. Large portions of the neighborhoods adjacent to our positions were on fire and the sounds of explosions and small arms fire were almost non-stop.

I remember looking at my watch and it read 11:24 pm.

I thought to myself, "I won't be alive to see the sun rise in the morning."

At that moment, I wasn't simply fearful of the risk of being killed, I was *convinced* that I was going to die. It was time to pray and I did so, while trying to maintain a look of calm and confidence on my face, lest the Marines with me see how worried I was about our chances of survival.

I wasn't married at the time and my thoughts drifted toward my family, especially my parents, knowing how hard my death was going to affect them. I can still remember the sensation of having a lump in my throat and feeling as if my body weighed a ton as I laid on the deck of the roof, thinking about what my parents were about to go through.

After several minutes, I had made peace with my fate and with God, with the genuine belief that I was about to meet him. To say that I was having a "religious experience" is an understatement.

But then I felt a sudden sense of peace and calm. As I laid next to a few of my Marines, I thought to myself, "Mike, if your time has come, so be it; at least go out like a Marine leader should—*leading!* Go see your Marines, because they need to see you right now."

I hurried down the building's staircase in total darkness, exited the lobby onto the street, and began running from position to position in the western portion of our sector, trying to time my runs to avoid incoming shells. Thankfully, the incoming artillery barrage had slowed a bit at this point, with perhaps only a few rounds impacting every couple of minutes or so. I stopped at several positions to talk with my Marines and encourage them. I distinctly remember entering a small bunker and seeing one of my young Marines, Private First Class Justin Glymph, who looked at me and said, "Sir, these bastards are trying to kill us!"

"It sure looks like it, Glymph!" I replied. "Keep your head down; I'll see you later." I then continued to move from position to position to see and talk with my Marines.

Our best hopes were realized, and we all miraculously survived that night. When morning came, the area adjacent to our perimeter was cloaked in dense smoke from the fires that the shelling had started. Some of the streets just outside of our position had collapsed and several heavily damaged cars were strewn about, with some of them still on fire.

I've kept in touch with many of the Marines I served with during this time. Even now, after all of these years, we inevitably end up talking about *"that night"* whenever we see each other.

And throughout my Marine Corps and business careers, whenever things became stressful and I found myself being a bit aggravated or disappointed, I'd look down at my watch and remember that night and how it felt to be "scared shitless"—knowing that my fate was literally hinging on the hope that an artillery shell or bullet did not have my name on it. Doing so would always quickly ground me in useful perspective. In my mind, I'd tell myself, "This really isn't that bad. Stop whining and start leading!"

I still have my watch and wear it every day. I don't ever want to forget the lessons, emotions, and "inner conversations" associated with the several "Rolex Moments" that I was privileged to have and fortunate to survive.

The Lesson

I often share this story when speaking to various groups about leadership, usually at the very end of the training session or seminar. I emphasize to them that as they focus on their professional goals and strive to become good leaders and climb the ladder of success, they will surely face many trials and tribulations.

The lesson I share with them is that while they navigate the many challenges and obstacles along their way, they should never forget that when it's all said and done, there is nothing more important in one's life than family and friends. I encourage them to keep their priorities in the proper order and to remain focused on what's really most important.

Many of my students and clients have already experienced their own Rolex Moments, and I am sure many reading this book have, too. I've no doubt that many of their experiences make mine look rather tame by comparison. I think all would agree that it's not a matter of *if* you will experience extremely challenging moments during your life, but *when*.

When a Rolex Moment happens to you, remember to do your duty to the best of your ability and, if possible, ask for the support of the people who love you.

And, as always . . . Lead by Example!

"When you arise in the morning, think of what a precious privilege it is to be alive— to breathe, to think, to enjoy, to love."

—MARCUS AURELIUS

Admiral James B. Stockdale

M any years ago, I became aware of the story of Admiral James B. Stockdale (1923 – 2005) and how he credited his understanding and application of Stoic philosophy as the main reason why he was able to endure and survive seven and a half years as a prisoner of war in North Vietnam. It was through reading about and learning from his experiences that I became convinced that there was something quite powerful about the insights and advice of the ancient Stoic philosophers. It would be impossible for any reader of this book to fully appreciate how I came to be an ardent follower and evangelist of Stoicism without knowing Admiral Stockdale's story.

Then Navy Captain Stockdale's plane was shot down over Vietnam in 1965, and during his seven and a half years of captivity he spent more than four years in solitary confinement. As a prisoner confined to Hoa Lo Prison—the infamous "Hanoi Hilton"—he was repeatedly subjected to various methods of torture techniques that included beatings, whippings, and near-asphyxiation with ropes. He was kept in solitary confinement, in total darkness, for four years, chained in heavy, abrasive leg irons for two years, malnourished due to a starvation diet, denied medical care, and deprived of letters from home in violation of the Geneva Convention.

Stockdale's Introduction to Stoicism

Stockdale discovered Stoicism as a "gray-haired" thirty-eight-year-old naval pilot in graduate school at Stanford University. He had become tired of the subject he'd enrolled to study, international relations, but became friends with the philosopher Philip Rhinelander, Dean of Humanities and Sciences, who took him under his wing. After a series of weekly tutorial sessions, Rhinelander handed Stockdale a book that would have a profound impact on him throughout the rest of his life. This book was a copy of The Enchiridion which was written by the Stoic philosopher Epictetus in 135 A.D.

Epictetus made a great impression on Stockdale, because instead of encouraging his followers to use empty rhetoric or abstract logic as they reflected upon their life's challenges, he encouraged them to use Stoic philosophy as a way of developing their minds. Stoicism could shape them in ways that would allow them to endure such misfortunes as imprisonment, torture, and exile, and ultimately teach them how to master their own fear of dying. Stockdale realized quickly that Stoicism had an immediate, positive effect on him and acknowledged that it had transformed his character and improved his life. He remarked that during this period, "I think it was obvious to my close friends, and certainly to me, that I was a changed man and, I have to say, a better man for my introduction to philosophy and especially to Epictetus."

Stockdale learned from Epictetus that a person's quest for happiness must be based upon a constant assessment of what is and is not within one's control. He understood that the ancient philosopher was teaching him that while he should try to influence fate, he must accept that he could not control it. Stoicism emphasizes that when fate strikes, the true measure of a person is their reaction to what fate has dealt him. Epictetus asserted that a person could either accept and adapt to what he couldn't change or he could be miserable as he wasted time and energy attempting to change things that simply were not able to be changed.

Stockdale also learned the importance of viewing difficult situations as an opportunity to act virtuously, and expecting that these situations would inevitably happen, instead of thinking and wishing that only good things and happiness were in one's future. He relished simple teachings by Epictetus such as, "Do not ask things to happen as you wish, but wish them to happen as they do happen, and your life will go smoothly."

During the next three years, as a squadron commander in the US navy, no matter what aircraft carrier he was aboard, what Stockdale called his "Epictetus books" were always by his bedside. By this he meant not only the Enchiridion and Discourses of Epictetus but also Xenophon's Memorabilia of Socrates and Homer's Iliad and Odyssey, all of which Stockdale considered essential reading for an understanding of Epictetus' Stoicism.

Stockdale as a Prisoner of War

During the initial phase of the Vietnam War, Stockdale was shot down over enemy territory and captured. Admiral Stockdale would later share the hardships he faced, experiences he lived through, and triumphs he attained through various speeches, interviews, and essays written throughout the years that followed his seven-year ordeal. These writings and compilations will follow later in the book—they are worth the read! He said of this experience:

"On September 9, 1965, I flew at 500 knots right into a flak trap, at tree-top level, in a little A-4 airplane—the cockpit walls not even three feet apart—which I couldn't steer after it was on fire, its control system shot out. After ejection I had about thirty seconds to make my last statement in freedom before I landed in the main street of a little village right ahead. And so help me, I whispered to myself: "Five years down there, at least. I'm leaving the world of technology and entering the world of Epictetus."

As he dropped from his snagged parachute into the jungle foliage, he clung to the teachings of the stoics he had studied and learned so much from. Immediately upon his descent, he was sieged upon by villagers who severely beat him and took him to be incarcerated in a prison camp for the next seven years.

Life in the prison camps of North Vietnam was unpleasant, difficult, and incredibly painful. All the prisoners were interrogated on a daily basis. At first Stockdale, as the senior officer imprisoned, was in charge of approximately fifty other prisoners; that number increased gradually through the months and years to over four hundred. The torture techniques utilized by the North Vietnamese were severe and intense and included "the ropes"—their arms would frequently be bound by ropes, with their arms behind their backs, and the ropes would be progressively tightened to the point that they could no longer breathe—fierce beatings, and waterboarding were common. In an effort to break the spirit of the prisoners they would often be kept in leg irons and isolation for months at a time.

For more than seven years Stockdale was subjected to the most extreme and oppressive circumstances. However, because of his knowledge and acceptance of the teachings of the Stoics, he was able to endure. He was able to accept that although he could not control the actions of his captors, he could in fact control how he chose to respond to them.

In 1993, in a speech delivered at the Great Hall, at King's College, Stockdale described his thoughts immediately after his plane was hit:

> . . . as I ejected from that airplane was the understanding that a Stoic always kept separate files in his mind for (A) those things that are "up to him" and (B) those things that are "not up to him." Another way of saying it is (A) those things that are "within his power" and (B) those things that are "beyond his power." Still another way of saying it is (A) those things that are within the grasp of "his Will, his Free Will" and (B) those things that are beyond it. All in category B are "external," beyond my control, ultimately dooming me to fear and anxiety if I covet them. All in category A are up to me, within my power, within my will, and properly subjects for my total concern and involvement. They include my opinions, my aims, my aversions, my own grief, my own joy, my judgments, my attitude about what is going on, my own good, and my own evil.

Stockdale added emphasis to his thoughts by saying: ". . . good and evil are not just abstractions you kick around and give lectures about and attribute to this person and that. The only good and evil that means anything is right in your own heart, within your will, within your power, where it's up to you." Or as Epictetus puts it in Chapter 32 of the Enchiridion, "Things that are not within our own power, not without our will, can by no means be either good or evil."

Stockdale finished his moving speech with a story about a note from a fellow prisoner that he received when he was returned to his cell after a particularly brutal torture session:

"Back in my cell, after the guard locked the door, I sat on my toilet bucket—where I could stealthily jettison the note if the peephole cover moved—and unfolded Hatcher's sheet of low-grade paper toweling on which, with a rat dropping, he had printed, without comment or signature, the last verse of Ernest Henley's poem Invictus:

'It matters not how strait the gate,
How charged with punishment the scroll,
I am the master of my fate:
I am the captain of my soul.'"

After Vietnam

For many years post-Vietnam, Stockdale shared his hard-earned lessons and truths with audiences as a college professor, college president, and senior research fellow at the Hoover Institution. He also reached the rank of vice admiral in the US Navy. In 1992 he even ran as a vice-president candidate alongside Ross Perot.

Thoughts of a Philosophical Fighter Pilot was published in 1995. It is a compilation of Stockdale's speeches and essays and embody his views on leadership, ethics, and resilience in military life. Although it isn't a well- known work, it depicts his knowledge gained through life's experiences in a unique way that is both impressive and inspiring.

It definitely validates the Stoic philosophers' views and teachings about how our mindset and the things we choose to focus on can help us endure even the most extreme hardships. I would highly recommend to anyone who is interested in Stoicism to read this book as well as his other publications: A Vietnam Experience (1984 Hoover Institution Press), Courage Under Fire (1993

Hoover Institution Press), and In Love and War—coauthored with his wife Sybil—(1990 Naval Institute Press).

His writings poignantly communicate his belief that any individual with the practiced and methodical development of a stoic mindset is capable of overcoming and rising triumphant despite facing adversity or struggling through hardships. James B. Stockdale died in 2005.

The Stockdale Paradox

A fter ejecting from his Douglas A-4 Skyhawk and drifting slowly in his parachute to the ground, Stockdale vowed to use what he knew would be years of captivity as a living laboratory for his study of Stoic philosophy:

Studying the life of Admiral Stockdale requires that one learn about what has become widely known as The Stockdale Paradox. First popularized by Jim Collins in his classic business book Good to Great, its essence is to emphasize why confronting reality is vital to success, and intelligently balancing realism and optimism in a dire situation is a key to success.

As mentioned in the previous chapter, during his time as a prisoner of war, Admiral Stockdale was repeatedly tortured and had no reason to believe he'd make it out alive. Once he accepted the grim reality of being imprisoned, he focused on embracing both the harshness of his situation with a balance of healthy optimism.

Stockdale explained this idea as the following: "You must never confuse faith that you will prevail in the end—which you can never afford to lose—with the discipline to confront the most brutal facts of your current reality, whatever they might be."

This quote by Stockdale is perhaps the most effective explanation of The Stockdale Paradox, the idea of hoping for the best outcome in a dire situation but acknowledging reality and preparing for the worst.

It was this contradictory way of thinking that enabled Stockdale to survive seven long years of captivity, torture, and solitary confinement.

Realism vs Optimism

During an interview with Collins for his book, Stockdale spoke about how the optimists fared as prisoners of war. When asked: "Who didn't make it out?," he replied without hesitation, "Oh, that's easy, the optimists." This confused Collins because Stockdale had minutes before told him that one must never lose faith in the possibility of prevailing against hardship, and he pressed the Admiral for clarity. Stockdale told him, "The optimists. Oh, they were the ones who said, 'We're going to be out by Christmas.' And Christmas would come, and Christmas would go. Then they'd say, 'We're going to be out by Easter.' And Easter would come, and Easter would go. And then Thanksgiving, and then it would be Christmas again. And they died of a broken heart."

Stockdale was trying to convey that those who allowed optimism to cloud the grim reality of their status as prisoners of war often went into a state of hopelessness that literally resulted in some of them dying.

"I never lost faith in the end of the story," he said, when I asked him. "I never doubted not only that I would get out, but also that I would prevail in the end and turn the experience into the defining event of my life, which in retrospect, I would not trade." – Jim Collins, *Good to Great*

Applying the Stockdale Paradox to your daily life

Thankfully, most of us will never face a situation in our life that comes close to that which he endured, but the Stockdale Paradox can add great value to a person's mindset and reactions to difficult situations in life.

It is fruitless to face difficult situations with anything other than logical assessment of the problem at hand. It doesn't do us any good to bury or ignore the reality that is in front of us when we encounter obstacles or adversity in our path. But neither is it productive to immediately throw our arms up in the air in hopeless despair.

What we need in order to emerge victorious on the other side of misfortune or difficulty is a balanced mentality that allows us to confidently hold on to a belief that there is always hope, while at the same time facing the immediate demands of the circumstances we are standing in.

I suppose in more modern terms you could refer to it as the ability to compartmentalize. You place the fragile sliver of hope in a vault in the most secure portions of your consciousness; and you make every bit of knowledge, intelligence, and skill available for dealing with the trial of making it through another moment.

Stockdale on Stoicism I: The Stoic Warrior's Triad

VADM James B. Stockdale, USN (Retired)

The views expressed in this report are those of the author and do not necessarily reflect the official policy or position of the Department of the Navy, the Department of Defense, or the U.S. Government. This report is approved for public release; distribution unlimited.

Foreword

With this publication, the Center for The Study of Professional Military Ethics inaugurates its "Occasional Paper" series, and we are genuinely proud to have Vice Admiral James B. Stockdale as the first author we publish. Indeed, we could have had no finer or more appropriate person with whom to launch this new Center program.

A 1947 graduate of the U.S. Naval Academy, Vice Admiral Stockdale is a figure of enormous stature among midshipmen more than a half century later, as a living embodiment of the Navy's core values—Honor, Courage, and Commitment. In late 1999, the Center hosted Admiral and Mrs. Stockdale for several days, including one major event—"Moral Courage: An Evening in Honor of Vice Admiral James B. Stockdale." Early in 2001, the Naval Academy Alumni Association announced that Admiral Stockdale had been selected to receive the Association's Distinguished Graduate Award. This prestigious award is given to a living graduate who has demonstrated a strong interest in supporting the Navy and the Naval Academy, has provided a lifetime of service to the nation, and has made significant contributions to the nation through public service.

A long-time student and teacher of philosophy, whose special focus is on the moral obligations of individuals, especially military officers, Admiral Stockdale asked last year if the Center would be interested in publishing some of his reflections on Stoicism and its influence on his life. We readily and enthusiastically agreed. The result will actually be our first two publications in this series, which we are calling *Stockdale on Stoicism I* and *Stockdale on Stoicism II*. The first, this publication, is a slightly edited version of two lectures Admiral Stockdale gave to the students at the U.S. Marine Corps Amphibious Warfare School in Quantico, Virginia on April 18, 1995. As you read this man's biography and his own words to those young Marine officers, you will no doubt conclude, as we have, that he is also the living embodiment of the Marine Corps motto, *Semper Fidelis*.

Albert C. Pierce
Director
Center for the Study of Professional Military Ethics
U.S. Naval Academy

37

Vice Admiral James B. Stockdale, USN, (RET.)

Vice Admiral Stockdale served on active duty in the regular Navy for 37 years, most of those years as a fighter pilot aboard aircraft carriers. Shot down on his third combat tour over North Vietnam, he was the senior naval prisoner of war in Hanoi for seven and one-half years—tortured 15 times, in solitary confinement for over four years, in leg irons for two.

When physical disability from combat wounds brought about Stockdale 's military retirement, he had the distinction of being the only three-star officer in the history of the U.S. Navy to wear both aviator wings and the Medal of Honor. Included in his 26 other combat decorations are two Distinguished Flying Crosses, three Distinguished Service Medals, four Silver Star medals, and two Purple Hearts.

As a civilian, Stockdale has been a college president (a year as President of The Citadel), a college teacher (a lecturer in the philosophy department of Stanford University), and a Senior Research Fellow at the Hoover Institution at Stanford for 15 years, a position from which he is now Emeritus. His writings all converge on the central theme of how man can rise in dignity to prevail in the face of adversity.

Besides numerous articles, he co-authored the book, In Love and War, with his wife, Sybil (Harper and Row, 1984), now in its second revised and updated edition (Naval Institute Press, 1990). NBC produced a dramatized version of this book which appeared in 1987, starring James Wood and Jane Alexander. Admiral Stockdale has also written two books of essays: *A Vietnam Experience: Ten Years of Reflection* (Hoover Press, 1984), and *Thoughts of a Philosophical Fighter Pilot* (Hoover Press, 1995). Both of the latter won the Freedom Foundation at Valley Forge's George Washington Honor Medal for books.

Upon his retirement from the Navy in 1979, the Secretary of the Navy established the Vice Admiral James Stockdale Award for Inspirational Leadership, which is presented annually to two commanding officers, one in the Atlantic Fleet and one in the Pacific Fleet. In 1989, Monmouth College in his native state of Illinois, from which he entered the Naval Academy, named its student union "Stockdale Center." The following year he was made a 1990 Laureate of the Abraham Lincoln Academy in Illinois in ceremonies at the University of Chicago. He is an Honorary Fellow in the Society of Experimental Test Pilots. In 1993 he was inducted into the Carrier Aviation Hall of Fame, and in 1995 was enshrined in the U.S. Naval Aviation Hall of Honor at the National Museum of Aviation in Pensacola, Florida.

Admiral Stockdale holds 11 honorary degrees.

The Stoic Warrior's Triad:
Tranquility, Fearlessness and Freedom

A lecture to the student body of
The Marine Amphibious Warfare School,
Quantico, Virginia
Tuesday, 18 April 1995

I feel at home here. I've flown combat with Marines in their own air planes—VMF2 12 out of Kaneohe. I was Wing commander of the carrier Oriskany on its 1965 cruise. One of our Fighter Squadrons was transitioning from F8 Crusaders to F4s. The gap was filled by the Marine F8 squadron. The skipper was Lieutenant Colonel Chuck Ludden, the Executive Officer was Major Ed Rutty, former Blue Angel. And my wingman in the squadron was a First Lieutenant named Duane Wills (later a Lieutenant General and head of Marine Corps Aviation). I spent 7½ years in prison with my shipmate Marine Captain Flarley Chapman, who was shot down two months after I was. So I'm in familiar territory, and damned glad to have spent 37 years in the Naval Service with the likes of guys like you.

Now, that said. I've got to choose my words well and get to the point if we are to get anything out of this morning. We're going to take some big steps right away. What kind of a racket is this military officership? Let's go right to the old master, Clausewitz. He said: "War is an act of violence to compel the enemy to do your will." Your will, not his will. We are in the business of breaking people's wills. That's all there is to war; once you have done that, the war is over.

And what is the most important weapon in breaking people's wills? This may surprise you, but I am convinced that holding the moral high ground is more important than firepower. For Clausewitz, war was not an activity governed by scientific laws, but a clash of *wills*, of *moral forces*. He wrote: "It is not the loss in men, horses, or guns, but in order, courage, confidence, cohesion and plan which come into consideration whether the engagement can still be continued; it is principally the *moral forces* which decide here." *Moral forces! Conviction! Mindgames!*

I had the wisdom of Clausewitz' stand on moral integrity demonstrated to me throughout a losing war as I sat on the sidelines in a Hanoi prison. To take a nation to war on the basis of any provocation that bears the smell of fraud is to risk losing national leadership's commitment when the going gets tough. When our soldiers' bodies start coming home in high numbers, and reverses in the field are discouraging, a guilty conscience in a top leader can become the Achilles heel of a whole country. Men of shame who know our road to war was not cricket are seldom those we can count on to hold fast, stay the course.

As some of you know, I led all three air actions in the Tonkin Gulf affair in the first week of August 1964. Moral corners were cut in Washington in our top leaders' interpretation of the events of August 4th at sea in order to get the Tonkin Gulf Resolution through Congress in a hurry. I was not only the sole eyewitness to all events, and leader of the American forces to boot; I was

41

cognizant of classified message traffic pertaining thereto. I knew for sure that our moral forces were squandered for short-range goals; others in the know at least suspected as much.

Mind games are important, and you have to play them honestly and seriously in this business. Clausewitz' battlefield enemy Napoleon not only agreed with his adversary, he made the same point of ethics in even more vivid terms. Napoleon said: "In war, the moral is to the physical as three is to one."

I'm going to concentrate on a *major* mind game today: Stoicism. Its seeds were planted in fourth century (B.C.) Athens, as a backlash against Plato's preoccupation with inuring everybody to the perfect society. Diogenes of Sinope, a friend of both Aristotle and Alexander the Great, (they all knew each other and all died within a two-year period), struck out on *his* campaign, not to conquer the East as did Alexander, not to stamp out ignorance as did Aristotle, but to do something about *man's* condition as a cowed citizen of a city state, without anything to believe in that could defuse the inner *fears and desires* which continually obsessed him. Man had to take command of his *inner self*, control himself. *The Stoic goal was not the good society, but the good man!*

And a lot of movements sprang up, mainly in the East, after the premature crumbling of Alexander the Great's empire in Asia after his early death; dozens of cults designed to improve men's *souls* organized themselves and headed West from Athens—among others Epicureans, of course the Stoics, and finally, almost bringing up the rear, the Christians.

To get my message today, you have only to have a general understanding of the message of one man: the Stoic philosopher Epictetus, *the* outstanding pagan moralist of the Roman Empire. I'll do my best to give you that understanding in a couple of 50-minute talks with a break in between. And for the remaining time, mainly through questions and answers, we'll discuss the worthiness of what I'll call Epictetus's *"Code of Conduct"* to be part of us as warriors. Code of Conduct? You thought Stoicism was a whole philosophy with a certain cosmology, a unique logic, a physics, a theory of knowledge, and all the rest? If so, you are right, it has all the accoutrements of a philosophy; it's just that Old Man Epictetus ignored everything about it except what it had to say about personal *conduct*, how the good *man* should *think*, and *behave*. "What do I care," Epictetus asked, "whether all existing things are composed of atoms, or of indivisibles, or of fire and earth? Is it not enough to learn the true nature of the *good and the evil?*"

The first principle of Stoicism is to live in harmony with nature—human nature and physical nature. My geneticist friend at Harvard, E. O. Wilson, tells me that the difference between men and animals is not reason, but human nature. Human nature is mostly genetically driven passions, passions designed to give us the capacity to survive and reproduce. It was David Hume who said, "Reason not only *is* but *ought to be* the slave of passions." *Physical* nature, the other half, is the physical universe and all its interactions. To the Stoic, physical nature is God's body. Have a look at yourself and see where you fit into the natural scheme of things. And play the part well.

Epictetus was impatient with unmanliness and loose living. He had a sarcasm that stripped affection bare. He had a fiery earnestness, which robbed his rude strokes of their cruelty. His message: "A man must think hard and live simply to do well."

I met old Epictetus back in graduate school in 1962. It was my great luck; in fact, it was a fluke that put us together. My favorite (philosophy) professor gave me one of Epictetus's books as a farewell present as I left to go back to sea. He had never mentioned him in class. Phil Rhinelander just thought Epictetus and I would make a good pair, and he was certainly right. I had never heard of Epictetus; in fact, today his name recognition is in about the third tier of philosophers. But his mind is *first tier*.

Everything I know about Epictetus I've developed *myself* over the years. It's been a one-on-one relationship. He's been in combat with me, leg irons with me, spent month-long stretches in blindfolds with me, has been in the ropes with me, has taught me that my *true business* is maintaining control over my moral purpose, in fact that my moral purpose is who I am. He taught me that I am totally responsible for everything I do and say; and that it is *I* who decides on and controls my own destruction and own deliverance. Not even God will intercede if He sees me throwing my life away. He wants me to be autonomous. He put *me* in charge of *me*. "It matters not how straight the gate, how charged with punishment the scroll. I am the master of my fate, I am the captain of my soul."

Don't be disturbed about my occasional references to the way the Stoics see God. He's the closest thing to the Christian God there is, according to Paul Tillich, a renowned Protestant theologian. Epictetus had heard of Christians, but he never knew any, nor were the Christians and the Stoics in competition in his lifetime. It was not until the latter part of the second century A.D. that a coherent Christian creed was beginning to emerge. Before that, nobody could state a cause *for* Christianity that would be intelligible to the pagan intellectual. The Stoics practiced a monotheistic religion from which Christianity borrowed much—the fatherhood of God and the brotherhood of man were well-established Stoic concepts before Christ was born; the Holy Ghost was a Stoic idea before Christ was born.

A quick thumbnail sketch of Epictetus's life goes like this: He was born to a Greek-speaking slave woman in a little town in Asia

Minor, up in the hills behind Ephesus about a hundred miles. At the time he was born, 50 A.D., that part of the world was a Roman colony with garrisoned troops. His mother's town, Hieopolos, was then and still is renowned for its natural hot springs and baths, and I think of it as probably an R and R spot for Roman troops. (I've visited there, of course.) Born to a slave, Epictetus was automatically a slave; he had a tough life. Crippled by a cruel master, he had a bad leg just like mine—left leg at the knee. When he was about 15, he was chained up and carried away in a slave caravan bound for Rome. He was bought at auction by a former slave, a "freedman" named Epaphroditus, secretary to the Emperor of Rome, the young (27-year-old) squirt Nero. Nero was bad and getting worse by the time young Epictetus moved into the Roman "White House." By the time Nero was 30, he had killed his half brother, his first wife, second wife, and mother. And he was letting the Empire run itself. The Roman Senate declared him a public enemy, and Epaphroditus was at Nero's side as the army was breaking down the door to arrest the Emperor. Nero tried to cut his own throat, muffed it, and Epaphroditus finished the job. Epaphroditus forever thereafter lived under a cloud, and Epictetus just took to the streets of Rome. A high-minded, intelligent, Greek-speaking, young man, he started attending philosophy lectures given in the public parks. And in those days in Rome, "philosophy" was synonymous with Stoicism.

The turning point in his life was his adoption by Musonius Rufus, the very best teacher of philosophy in first-century Rome. Though Epictetus was still technically a slave, Rufus, an Etruscan knight, took him as a student. Rufus was as fluent in Greek as he was in Latin, and he and Epictetus got on well. In one passage, Epictetus tells of his tutor's mastery of seminar instruction: "Rufus spoke in such a way that each of us, as we sat there, fancied someone had gone to him and told him of our faults; so effective was his grasp of what men actually do and think. So vividly did he set before each man's eyes his particular weakness."

Epictetus's tutelage ran on for at least 10 years, and then Rufus launched him on a career as a bonafide philosopher of Rome. Epictetus, like all philosophers in Rome, was exiled by Emperor Domitian in the year 89 A.D., and he picked out a little town of Nicopolis (where I've also been), on the Adriatic coast of Greece, as a place to found a school. My favorite authorities set the date of his death at 138 A.D., at age 88. I've come across nothing about his "retirement," so I think of him as starting his school in about 90 A. D. at age 40, and teaching there for another 40 or 50 years. This little book like the one I got from my professor in 1962 is called *The Enchiridion*, meaning in Greek "ready at hand." It is only selected excerpts from eight volumes of Epictetus's lectures and conversations given, we think, in the year 108 A.D. He was talking to basically rich, young men from formidable families, mostly from Athens and Rome. It was the Socrates scene all over again, 500 years later—the same students, same age, mid-20s, the same type of dialogue.

Epictetus, a bachelor until his very late years when he took a wife his age to help him care for an infant he rescued from death by "exposure," was a "natural," extraordinarily gifted teacher. He was gregarious—never missed the Olympic games which were conducted only about 50 miles from his school. He talks about the Olympics of those years in *Enchiridion* [29]:

> In every affair, consider what precedes and what follows, and then undertake it. Otherwise you will begin with spirit, indeed, careless of the consequences, and when these are developed, you will shamefully desist. I would conquer at the Olympic Games. But

consider what precedes and what follows, and then, if it be for your advantage, engage in the affair. You must conform to rules, submit to a diet, refrain from dainties; exercise your body, whether you choose it or not, at a stated hour, in heat and cold; you must drink no cold water, and sometimes no wine. In a word, you must give yourself up to your trainer as to a physician. Then, in the combat, you may be thrown into a ditch, dislocate your arm, turn your ankle, swallow an abundance of dust, receive stripes [for negligence], and after all, lose the victory. When you have reckoned up all this, if your inclination still holds, set about the combat.

The religious possibilities of Stoicism were developed further by Epictetus than by any of his Stoic predecessors over the previous 400 years. But his manner of speaking was *not* that of a prissy moralist. He often phrased his pithy remarks in the athletic metaphor: "Difficulties are what show men's character. Therefore when a difficult crisis meets you, remember that you are as the raw youth, with whom God-the-trainer is wrestling." And in a prayer to God, he uses the military metaphor: "If Thou sendest me to a place where men have no means of living in accordance with nature, I shall depart this life, not in disobedience to Thee, but as though Thou were *sounding for me the recall.*" The Stoics accepted suicide, under certain conditions.

And he was funny. Funny, even as he played the part of shock psychologist! He asks and answers the question: What do you do for friends as you ascend the ladder of intellectual sophistication? Do you hang in with your old pals, or concentrate on intellectual peers? "If you do not drink with old friends as you used to drink with them, you cannot be loved by them as much. So choose whether you want to be a boozer and likeable to them, or sober and not likeable." Then he makes it clear that in *his* mind, satisfaction and self-respect are best served by escalating friendships apace with your education. "But if that does not please you, turn about the whole of you, to the opposite; become one of the addicts to unnatural vice, one of the adulterers, and act in corresponding fashion. Yes, and jump up and shout your applause to the dancer!"

To the painfully shy and reticent student:

> As the good chorus singers do not render solos, but sing perfectly well with a number of other voices, so some men cannot walk around by themselves. Man, if you are anybody, both walk around by yourself, and talk to yourself, and don't hide yourself in the chorus. Let yourself be laughed at sometimes, look about you, shake yourself up, so as to at least find out who you actually are!

Now neither these eight volumes of Epictetus "lectures," hallway talk, and private conversations, *nor* their "executive summary," *The Enchiridion*, were compiled by Epictetus. He couldn't have cared less about being in print. They were taken down in some kind of frantic shorthand by a 23-year-old student, a remarkable man, Flavius Arrianus, usually known as just Arrian. He was an aristocratic Greek born in a Black Sea province of Asia Minor. You can't help but imagine what it took for him to improvise this shorthand and follow the old man around and take down all that material. After getting a load of Epictetus and his "living" speech, he must have said something like: "Wow, we've got to get this guy down on papyrus!" In his dedication of his final manuscript to a friend, he writes: "Whatever I heard him say, I used to write down, word for word, as best I could, endeavouring to preserve it as a memorial, for my own future use, of his way of thinking and the frankness of his speech. Let those who read these words be assured of this: that when Epictetus *spoke* them, the hearer could not help but feel exactly what Epictetus *wanted* him to feel."

That is the mark of a good teacher!

Arrian was a writer throughout his life. His last and largest book was his definitive text on Alexander the Great's expedition to the east: *The Anabasis of Alexander*. Some time after his death, four of his eight volumes of Epictetus disappeared. During the Middle Ages the four remaining were bound under the title Epictetus's *Discourses*. As I said, *The Enchiridion* was tidbits from all eight volumes, so you'll find things in *The Enchiridion* that are not in *Discourses*.

History gives us snapshots of Arrian's other activities in his illustrious career. After leaving Epictetus's school, and a term as a successful Roman army officer, we find him lecturing in Athens in about 120 A.D., and there meeting Roman Emperor Hadrian, who was about to start a five-year tour of the Empire following his investiture in 117 A.D. Epictetus figured into two fallouts of Arrian's presence in Athens in the years following. Hadrian, in 130 A.D., appointed Arrian consul for a year, followed by six years as governor of the large province of Cappadocia in Asia Minor. Arrian introduced Epictetus to Emperor Hadrian and they became lifetime friends. Secondly, when Arrian vacated his lectureship in Athens for politics, he was relieved by a Q. Janius Rusticus, who later became the tutor to the young Marcus Aurelius. Later, in his book *Meditations*, a book on Stoicism, Emperor Marcus Aurelius acknowledged his debt to Epictetus for the wisdom he gained from studying his eight volumes as a youth. (Rusticus had some copies Arrian left him and gave one to his student, young Aurelius.)

So this slave boy who became a schoolmaster, gained fame as a respected scholar in the highest circles of the only superpower of the ancient world. And those were important years in world history. They are the years the English historian Edward Gibbon was talking about in the famous statement in his book, *The History of the Decline and Fall of the Roman Empire*: "If a man were called upon to fix the period in the history of the world during which the condition of the human race was most happy and prosperous, he would without hesitation name that which elapsed from the accession of Nerva to the death of Marcus Aurelius." That comes to a period of 84 years, from 96 A.D. to 180 A.D. "Their united reigns are possibly the only period in history in which the happiness of a great people was the sole object of government."

The eminent old philosopher Will Durant, in the volume named "Caesar and Christ" in his *History of Civilization* series, calls the five emperors spanning the era that Gibbon admired, "the philosopher kings." All were Stoics or had strong Stoic sympathies: Nerva pardoned exiled Stoics of the Domitian reign. Trajan had a Stoic tutor in his quarters. Hadrian was Epictetus's close friend. Antonius Pius, a "product of the Stoic school," insisted that in Roman law courts, Stoic legal principles be followed, i.e. that (1) in all cases of doubt, judgments be resolved in favor of the accused, and (2) a man should be held innocent until proven guilty. And the last of the philosopher kings, Marcus Aurelius, probably the finest of all Roman Emperors, secretly wrote his Stoic *Meditations* by candlelight in his tent perched on one or another of the mountainsides of Germany, where for the last 12 years of his life he was in the field as Commanding General of the Roman armies, continually engaged in defending the northern frontiers of the Empire against tribal attacks.

The Roman Stoic was more a man of action than contemplation, but listen to the paragraph of old soldier Aurelius on how to die: "Pass this little space of time—your lifetime—comfortably, with nature, and end thy journey in contentment, like the ripe olive that falls, praising the earth that gave birth to it, and thanking the tree that made it grow."

On the question of afterlife, Marcus Aurelius took up and emphasized the teaching of Epictetus. They alone, among Stoics, were very careful in what they said about death. There was no proof of afterlife, and rather than possibly mislead people, they refrained from the more ample language of their predecessors. Matthew Arnold described Marcus Aurelius as "perhaps, the most beautiful figure in history."

The five Stoic philosopher kings were the sort of men you would want to have as Marine Corps Commandants. A few notes from my history books: The second of the five, Trajan, was Commanding General of the Roman army in Cologne when he was notified that Emperor Galba had died, and that *his* number was up. He was Emperor for 19 years, and throughout, habitually wore his army uniform. Tall and robust, he was wont to march on foot with his troops and ford, with full kit, the hundreds of rivers they crossed.

Let me tell you about that five-year trip his successor, Emperor/General Hadrian, took after meeting Arrian in Athens. Accompanied by experts, architects, builders, and engineers, he had left Rome in 121 A.D. to inspect defenses in Germany. He lived the life of his soldiers, eating their fare, never using a vehicle, walking with full military equipment 20 miles at a time. The Roman army was never in better condition than in his reign. He traveled the Rhine to its mouth, sailed to Britain, ordered the building of a wall from Solway Firth to the mouth of the Tyne "to divide the barbarians [Scots] from the Romans [in England]"—"Hadrian's Wall." Back to Gaul, then to Spain, then down into Northwest Africa where he led some garrisoned Roman Legions against Moors who had been raiding the Roman towns of Mauretania. That finished, he boarded one of his Mediterranean warships and went to Ephesus, went up and inspected the ports of the Black Sea, back down to Rhodes, and still curious at 50, stopped in Sicily and climbed Mt. Etna to see the sunrise from a perch 11,000 feet above his Mediterranean Sea.

* * * *

The time interval between my finishing graduate school and becoming a prisoner was almost exactly three years, September 1962 to September 1965. That was a very eventful period in my life. I started a war (led the first-ever American bombing raid on North Vietnam), led good men in about 150 aerial combat missions in flak, and throughout three 7-month cruises to Vietnam I had not only the *Enchiridion*, but the *Discourses* on my bedside table on each of the three aircraft carriers I flew from. And I read them.

On the 9th of September 1965, 1 flew right into a flak trap, at tree-top level, 500 knots, in a little A-4 airplane—cockpit walls not even three feet apart—which I couldn't steer after it was on fire, control system shot out. After ejection I had about 30 seconds to make my last statement in freedom before I landed on the main street of that little village right ahead. And so help me, I whispered to myself: "Five years down there at least. I'm leaving the world of technology and entering the world of Epicetus."

I want to step off the chronology escalator for just a minute and explain what memories of the *Enchiridion* and *Discourses* I did have "ready at hand" when I ejected from that plane. What I had in hand was the understanding that the Stoic, particularly the disciple of Epictetus who developed this accounting, always keeps separate files in his mind for: (a) those things which are "up to him" and (b)

52

those things which are "not up to him;" or another way of saying it, (a) those things which are "within his power" and (b) those things which are "beyond his power;" or still another way of saying it: (a) those things which are within the grasp of "his will, his free will," and (b) those things which are beyond it. Among the relatively few things that are "up to me, within my power," within my will, are my opinions, my aims, my aversions, my own grief, my own joy, my moral purpose or will, my attitude toward what is going on, my own good, and my own evil. Please note: All these things, as are all things of real importance to the Stoic, are matters that apply *principally* to your *"inner self,"* where you *live.*

Now I'm talking like a preacher here for a bit. Please understand that I'm not trying to *sell* anything; it's just the most efficient way to explain it. Stoicism is one of those things that, when described analytically, sounds horrible to some modem people. Stoic scholars agree that to describe it effectively, the teacher must "become, for the time being at least," a Stoic.

For instance, to give you a better feel for why "your own good and your own evil" are on the list, I want to quote Alexander Solzhenitsyn from his book *Gulag Archipelago*, when he talks about that point in prison when he gets his act together, realizes his residual powers, and starts what I know as "ascending," riding the updrafts of occasional euphoria as you realize you are getting to know yourself and the world for the first time.

> It was only when I lay there on the rotting prison straw that I sensed within myself the first stirrings of *good.* Gradually it was disclosed to me that the line separating good and evil passes not between states nor between social classes nor between political parties, but right through every human heart, through all human hearts. And that is why I turn back to the

years of my imprisonment and say, sometimes to the astonishment of those about me, bless you, prison, for having been a part of my life.

I *understand* that. He learned, as I and many others have learned, that good and evil are not just abstractions that you kick around and give lectures about, and attribute to this person and that. The only good or evil that mean anything are right in your own heart: within your will, within your power, where it's up to you. What the Stoics say is: "You take care of that, and you'll have your hands full."

What is not up to you? Beyond your power? Not subject to your will in the last instance? For starters, let's take "your station in life." As I glide down toward that little town on my short parachute ride, I'm just about to learn how negligible is my control over my station in life. It's not at all up to me. Of course I'm going right now from being the Wing Commander, in charge of a thousand people (pilots, crewmen, maintenance men), responsible for nearly a hundred airplanes, and beneficiary of goodness knows all sorts of symbolic status and goodwill, to being an object of contempt. "Criminal," I'll be known as. But that's not *half* the revelation that is the realization of your own *fragility*, that you can be reduced by the natural elements, or men, to a helpless, sobbing wreck—unable to control even your own bowels—in a matter of minutes. And more than that even, you're going to face fragilities you never before let yourself believe could be true. Like after mere minutes, in a flurry of action while being knocked down and then sat up to be bound with tourniquet-tight ropes, with care, by a professional, hands cuffed behind, jack-knifed forward, head pushed down between your ankles held secure in lugs attached to a heavy iron bar, that with the onrush of anxiety, knowing your upper-body blood circulation has been stopped, and feeling the evergrowing pain and the ever-closing-in of claustrophobia as the man standing on your back gives your head one last shove down with his heel and you start to gasp and vomit, that you can be made to blurt out answers, probably correct answers, to questions about anything they know you know. I'm not going to pull you through that explanation again. I'll just call it "taking the ropes."

No, "station in life" can be changed from that of a dignified and competent gentleman of culture to that of a panic-stricken, sobbing, self-loathing wreck, maybe a *permanent* wreck if you have no *will*, in less than an hour. So what? So after you work a lifetime to get yourself all set up, and then delude yourself into thinking that you have some kind of ownership claim on your station in life, you're riding for a fall. You're asking for disappointment. To avoid that, stop kidding yourself, just do the best you can on a common-sense basis to make your station in life what you want it to be, but never get *hooked* on it. Make sure in your heart of hearts, in your inner self, that you treat your station in life with *indifference*. Not with contempt, only with indifference.

And so on to a long list of things which some unreflective people assume they're assured of controlling to the last instance—your reputation, for example. Do what you will, it's at least as fickle as your station in life. *Others* decide what your reputation is. Try to make it as good as possible, but *again*, don't get *hooked* on it. In your heart, when you get out the key and open up that old rolltop desk where you really keep your stuff, don't let "reputation" get mixed up with what's within your *moral purpose*, what's within the power of your *will*, in other words, what's up to *you*. Make sure it's in the bottom drawer, filed under "matters of indifference." And so too with your *health*, your *wealth*, your *pleasure*, your *pain*, your *fame*, your *disrepute*, your *life*, and your *death*. They are all *externals*, all outside your control in the last instance, all outside the power of where you really live. And where you really live is confined to the regime of your moral purpose, confined to matters that can be projected by your acts of will—like desires, aims, aversions, judgments, attitudes, and of course, your good and your evil. For a Stoic, the moral purpose, the will, is the only repository of things of absolute value. Whether they are projected wisely or foolishly, for good or for evil, is up to you. When his will is set on the right course, a man becomes good; when it's on a foul course, he becomes evil. With the right course comes good luck and happiness, and with the foul course, bad luck and misery.

To a Stoic, bad luck is your fault; you've become *addicted* to *externals*. Epictetus: "What are tragedies, but the portrayal in tragic verse of the sufferings of men who have admired things external?" Not even God will intercede in your decisions. Epictetus:

> God gives you attributes, like magnanimity, courage, and endurance, to enable you to bear whatever happens. These are given free of all restraint, compulsion, or hindrance; He has put the whole matter under your control without reserving even for Himself any power to prevent or hinder.

As I have said, your deliverance and your destruction are 100 percent *up to you*.

I know the difficulties of gulping all this down right away. You keep thinking of practical problems. Everybody has to play the game of life. You can't just walk around saying: "I don't care about my health, or wealth, or my reputation, or whether I'm sent to prison or not." Epictetus was a great teacher because he could draw a word picture that cleared up the way to look at what he was talking about.

In this case, Epictetus said everybody should play the game of life—that the best play it with "skill, form, speed and grace." But like most games, you play it with a ball. Your team devotes all its energies to getting the ball across the line. But after the game, what do you do with the ball? Nobody much cares. It's not worth anything. The competition, the game, was the thing. You play the game with care, making sure you are never making the external a part of yourself, but merely lavishing your skill in regard to it. The ball was just "used" to make the game possible, so just roll it under the porch and forget it, let it wait for the next game. Most important of all, just don't *covet* it, don't *seek* it, don't *set your heart on it*. It is this latter route that makes externals dangerous, makes them the route to slavery. First you covet or abhor "things," and then along comes he who can confer or remove them. I quote *Enchiridion* (*The Little Book*) 14: "A man's master is he who is able to confer or remove whatever that man seeks or shuns. Whoever then would be free, let him wish nothing, let him decline nothing, which depends on others, else he must necessarily become a slave." *Discourses* 1/121: "Who is your master? He who has authority over any of the things upon which you have set your heart." These last quotations constitute the real core of what a person needs in order to understand the POW situation.

So I took those core thoughts into prison. I also remembered a lot of attitude-shaping remarks from the *Enchiridion* on how not to kid yourself into thinking that you can somehow stand aloof, be an "observer of the passing scene," aloof from the prisoner underground organization. *Enchiridion* 17:

> Remember that you are an actor in a drama of such
> sort as the Author chooses: if short, then in a short
> one; if long, then in a long one. If it be His pleasure
> that you should enact a poor man, or a cripple, or a

ruler, or a private citizen, see that you act it well. For this is your business, to act well the given part. But to choose it belongs to Another.

The capital A's on Author and Another are Stoic code markings for "another name for God." Our minds are part of the Divine Mind of God; it is like a flame, and individual consciousnesses are sparks in it. Conversely, we are fragments of God; each one of us has within us a part of Him. We're part of God and he's part of us.

Another attitude-shaping remark: When in tight straits, you should stifle what's in you of that Student Body President personality, of give-and-take, openness, being responsive, offering counter-options rather than outright refusal to go along. We called people who acted like student body presidents "players" in prison, and tried to prevent them from digging their own graves. *Enchiridion* 28: "If a person had delivered up your body to some passer-by, you would certainly be angry. And do you feel no shame in delivering up your own mind to any reviler?"

All that, over those three years (between graduate school and being shot down), I had put away for the future. Right now, and I'm back on chronology, it's very *quiet* in a parachute, and I can hear the rifle shots down below and can match them up with bullet rips occurring in the parachute canopy above me. Then I can hear the noontime shouting and see the fists waving in the town as my chute hooks a tree but deposits me on a main street in good shape. With two quick-release fastener flips, I'm free of the chute, and immediately gang-tackled by the 10 or 15 town roughnecks I had seen in my peripheral vision, pounding up the street from my right. It felt to me like the quarterback sack of the century. I don't want to make a big thing of this, nor indicate that I was surprised at my reception, but by the time the tackling and pummeling and twisting and wrenching were over, and it lasted for three or more minutes before the guy in the pith helmet got there to blow his whistle, I had a very badly broken leg that I felt sure would be with me for life. And that hunch turned out to be right. And I'll have to say that I felt only minor relief when I hazily recalled crippled Epictetus's admonition in *Enchiridion* 9: "Lameness is an impediment to the leg, but not to the *will*; and say this to yourself with regard to everything that happens. For you will find it to be an impediment to something else, but not truly to *yourself*."

As an insider, I knew that whole setup on POWs: that the North Vietnamese already held about 30 prisoners in that early September 1965, probably up in Hanoi; that I was the only Wing Commander, Navy or Air Force, to survive an ejection; and that I would be their senior, their Commanding Officer, and would remain so, very likely, throughout this war, which I felt sure would last at least five years. And here I was starting off crippled and flat on my back.

Well, Epictetus turned out to be right. After a crude operation just to get my knee locked and splayed leg under me, I was on crutches within a couple of months. And the crooked leg, healing itself, was strong enough to hold me up without crutches in a few more. I took command (clandestinely, of course) of the by-then 75 pilots—due to grow to 466 over the 7½ years—determined "to play well the given part."

* * * *

I'll drop the prison chronology right there, and concentrate on bringing to light as many more interesting wrinkles of Epictetus and his Stoicism as time will allow.

I would like to say straight off that I have read through and studied the *Discourses*, at least 10 times, to say nothing of my many excursions into the *Enchiridion*, and I have never found a single inconsistency in Epictetus's code of tenets. It is a put-together package, free of contradictions. The old boy may or may not appeal to you, but if he turns you off, don't blame it on incoherence; Epictetus has no problem with logic.

I think more needs to be said about good and evil. After all, the *Stoic is indifferent to everything but* good and evil. In Stoic thought, our good and our evil come from the same locus. "Vice and virtue reside in the will alone." "The essence of good and evil lies in an attitude of the will." Solzhenitsyn locates it in the heart, and Epictetus would buy that, or *will*, or *moral purpose*, or *character*, or *soul*, he's not a nitpicker about things like that. What he bears down on is that your good and your evil are the essence of *you*. You *are* moral purpose. You *are* rational will. You are not hair, you are not skin, you are moral purpose—get that beautiful, and you will be beautiful.

That was revealed to Solzhenitsyn when he felt within himself the first stirrings of good. And in that chapter, the old Russian elaborated other truths about good and evil. Not only does the line separating them *not* pass between political or cultural or ethnic groupings, but right through every human heart, through *all* human hearts, he adds that for any individual over the years, this separation line within the heart shifts, oscillates somewhat. That even in hearts *overwhelmed* by evil, one small bridgehead to *good* is retained. And even in the *best* of all hearts, there remains an *unuprooted* small corner of evil. There is some good and some evil in all of us, and that's Stoic doctrine. In that same chapter, Solzhenitsyn comments: "If only there were evil people somewhere insidiously committing evil deeds, and it were necessary only to separate them from the rest of us and destroy them. But the line dividing good and evil cuts through the heart of every human being, and who is willing to destroy a piece of his own heart?"

I just want you to know that I connect with that. In a crucible like a torture prison, you reflect, you silently study what makes those about you tick. Once I had taken the measure of my torture guard, watched his eyes as he worked, watched him move, *felt* him move as he stood on my slumped-over back and cinched up the ropes pulling my shoulders together, I came to know that there was good in him. That was ironic because when he first came in with the new commissar when torture was instigated after I got there, I had nicknamed him "Pigeye" because of the total vacancy of the stare of the one eye he presented as he peeked through cell door peepholes. He was my age, balding and wiry, quick, lithe and strong, like an athletic trainer. He was totally emotionless, thus his emotionless eyes. He had almost no English-language capability, just motions and grunts. Under orders, he put me through the ropes 15 times over the years, and rebroke my bad leg once, I feel sure inadvertently. It was a court martial scene and he was having to give me the ropes before a board of North Vietnamese officers. The officers sat at a long table before Pigeye and me, and behind us was a semi-circle of soldiers bearing rifles with fixed bayonets at a kind of "dangle" position, the bayonet pointing at the cement floor ahead of them. This was in the "knobby" torture room of "New Guy Village" at Hoa Lo prison in August 1967— so-called because the walls had been crudely speckled with blobs of cement the size of an ice cream scoop in a "soundproofing" attempt. I could tell Pigeye was nervous because of these officers whom I had never seen before, and I don't think he had, and he pressed me flat over my bad leg instead of the good one he had always put the tension on before. The healing knee cartilage gave way with a loud "pop," and the officers looked at each other and then got up and left. I couldn't get off that floor and onto my feet for nearly two months.

In all those years, we probably had no more than 24 hours, one-on-one together. But neither of us ever broke the code of an unvaryingly strict "line of duty" relationship. He never tricked me, always played it straight, and I begged no mercy. I admired that in him, and I could tell he did in me. And when people say: "He was a torturer, didn't you *hate* him?" I say, like Solzehnitsyn, to the astonishment of those about me, "No, he was a good soldier, never overstepped his line of duty."

By that time, I had learned that *fear* and *guilt* are the real pincers that break men's wills. I would chant under my breath as I was marched to interrogation, knowing that I must refuse to comply, and take the ropes: "Your eyes must show no fear; they must show no guilt." The North Vietnamese had learned never to take a prisoner "downtown"—to the payoff for what our whole treatment regime was about—public propaganda exploitation—unless he was truly intimidated, unless they were *sure* he felt *fear*. Their threats had no meaning unless you felt *fear*. They had suffered the political damage of several, including myself, who had acted up, spoken up, and blurted out the truth to the hand-picked audience of foreigners at the press conference. Book IV of *Discourses*: "When a man who has set his will neither on dying nor upon living at any cost, comes into the presence of the tyrant, what is there to prevent him from being without fear? Nothing."

Fear is an *emotion*, and controlling your emotions can be *empowering*.

I think I have mentioned all the things that the Stoics thought were truly "in our power," within the realm of our moral purpose, under the control of our free will, save one category. It requires a little different thinking, so I've saved it for last. I have introduced it already, in part. The Stoics believed that all human *emotions* are acts of will. You're happy because you want to be happy, you're drained or sad when you want to be sad, and fear is *not* something that danger forces on you. When you find yourself afraid, it's time to realize that you decided, wanted, willed that you fear. As I said above, without your having fear, nobody can meaningfully threaten you. In *Discourses*, there is a dialogue something like this, and it was like old home week to me:

> When questioned, I had to give him our escape plans; he threatened me with death; I was compelled, I had no choice. . . .That's not right; you had a choice and you made it. It may have been justified, I won't judge that for now. But be honest with yourself. Don't say you had to do *anything* just because you are threatened with death. You simply decided it was better to comply. It was *your will* that compelled you. *Refuse to want to fear and you start acquiring a constancy of character that makes it impossible for another to do you wrong.* Threats have no effect unless you *fear*.

Epictetus says: "Will you then realize that this *epitome* of all the ills that befall man, of his ignoble spirit, of his cowardice, is not *death*, but rather his *fear of death*."

As I said, learning to take charge of your emotions is *empowering*. When you get there, *Enchiridion* 30 applies: "No one can harm you without your permission." And by "harm" Epictetus means, as Stoics always mean, harming your inner self, your self-respect, and your obligation to be faithful. He can break your arm or your leg, but not to worry. They'll heal.

What are some of the guidelines to identifying the good and the evil in Stoic thought?

Well, first, Stoicism goes back to the idea that nature is God's body, and that it doesn't do to try to improve on it. In fact, God and Nature are two aspects of the same thing. God's Soul is the Mind of the universe, and Nature is his body. Just as the Mind is the active, and Nature is the passive, so our minds are active and our bodies passive. Mind over matter; it all happens in your head, so don't worry about your body. The perfect man models himself on this operation of the universe. Nothing is ever lost. All remains in the care of Providence. Just as the universe, in which the Mind of God is imminent and indwelling and moves in a manner self-sufficient and self-ruling, *so the good man is independent, autonomous, a law unto himself, and a follower of the eternal guidance of duty and conscience.*

This is called the coherence of Stoicism, and Cicero used this as the basis of his founding of Natural Law and International Law. "True law is right reason in agreement with nature."

The Stoics were good citizens. In politics the Stoic would love his country and hold himself ready to die at any time to avert *its* disgrace or *his own*. But a man's conscience was to be higher than *any* law. A man has a right to be responsible, self-ruling, autonomous.

So on good and evil, where does that leave us? Nothing that is natural can be evil. Death cannot be evil. Disease cannot be evil. Natural disasters cannot be evil. Nothing *inevitable* can be evil. The universe as a whole is perfect, and everything in it has a place in the overall design. Inevitability is produced by the workings of this mechanism. Events do not happen by chance, they arrive by appointment. There is a cause for everything, and "chance" is simply a name for undiscovered causes.

Neither good nor evil can be abstractions. Epictetus said: "Where do I look for the good and the evil? *Within me*, in that which is my own." But for that which is another's *never* employ the words "good" or "evil," or anything of the sort. Goods and evils can *never* be things others do to you, or for you.

Why not make health or life be good? Because man *deserves the good*, and it's better that he not "deserve" anything he does not control; otherwise, he will go after what is not his, and this is the start of crime, wars, you name it.

Another thing. You do not control God. You must not refer to Him as "good" or "evil." Why not? If you pin these mundane terms on Him, reciting "God is good," people may become tempted, when things God controls run counter to what they're trying to do—weather being unfavorable for farmers or the wind being from the wrong direction for sailors—to start calling Him evil, too. And that's impious. Remember, says Epictetus: "Piety must be preserved. Unless piety and self-interest be conjoined, piety cannot be maintained in any man."

Now [let me close with] some other things that follow from the assumptions of Stoicism that you might not have thought of. The Stoics say that the invincible man is he who cannot be dismayed by any happening outside of his span of control, outside his will, his moral purpose. Does this sound irresponsible to you? Here you have a man who pays no attention as the world blows up around him, so long as he had no part in causing it.

The answer to that depends on whether or not you believe in collective guilt. The Stoics do not. Here is what *The Encyclopedia of Philosophy* says about collective guilt:

> If guilt, in the proper sense, turns on deliberate wrongdoing, it seems that no one can be guilty for the act of another person—there can be no shared or collective or universal guilt. Guilt is incurred by the free choice of the individual. . . . But many have questioned this. Among them are some sociologists

who misrepresent in this way the dependence of the individual on society. But the main location of the idea of collective guilt is religion—many forms of doctrines of original sin and universal sin regard guilt as a pervasive state of mankind as a whole.

Speaking for myself, I think of collective guilt as a manipulative tool. It reminds me of the communist "criticism/self-criticism" technique. Many of the precepts of the Stoics depend on an abhorrence of the concept of collective guilt.

The Stoics believe that every man bears the exclusive responsibility *himself* for his own good and his own evil—and that leads to their further conclusion that *it is impossible to imagine a moral order in which one person does the wrong, and another, the innocent, suffers.* Now add all that to Epictetus's firm belief that we are all born with an *innate* conception of good and evil, and what is noble and what is shameful, what is becoming and unbecoming, what is fitting and inappropriate, what is right to do and what is wrong, and further, remembering that all Stoic talk refers to the inner man, what is going on "way down in here." It follows that the perpetrator of evil pays the full price for his misdeed in suffering the injury of knowing that he has destroyed the good man with him. Man has "moral sense," and he reaps the benefits and pays the price for this inheritance.

This self-knowledge that you have betrayed yourself, destroyed yourself, is the very worst harm that can befall a Stoic. Epictetus says:

- "No one comes to his fall because of another's deed."
- "No one is evil without loss or damage."
- "No man can do wrong with impunity."

I call this whole personal guilt package that Epictetus relied upon, "the reliability of the retribution of the guilty conscience." As I sometimes say, "There can be no such thing as a 'victim;' you can only be a 'victim' of yourself." Remember:

- Controlling your emotions can be empowering.
- Your inner self is what you make it.
- Refuse to want to fear, and you start acquiring a constancy of character that makes it impossible for another to do you wrong.

Somebody asked Epictetus: "What is the fruit of all these doctrines?" He answered with three sharp words: "Tranquility, Fearlessness, and Freedom."

Thank you.

Stockdale on Stoicism II:
Master of My Fate

VADM James B. Stockdale, USN (Retired)

Foreword

This is the second in a series of Occasional Papers published by the Center for the Study of Professional Military Ethics. It shares with the first occasional paper a common author—Vice Admiral James B. Stockdale—and a common theme—the influence of Stoic philosophy on Admiral Stockdale's life and career.

As you read these two papers, you will realize that Admiral Stockdale's own description of himself (in the title of one of his books) rings true: He *is* a "philosophical fighter pilot."

In this second paper, Admiral Stockdale takes us deeply, perhaps uncomfortably deeply, into the Hanoi prison where he was held captive for seven and one-half years. This is Stoicism in practice, not just in theory. It is *living* philosophy, not just teaching it. This is *applied* ethics, not merely ethics in theory.

Early in 2001, the Naval Academy Alumni Association announced that Admiral Stockdale had been selected to receive the Association's Distinguished Graduate Award. This prestigious award is given to a living graduate who has demonstrated a strong interest in supporting the Navy and the Naval Academy, has provided a lifetime of service to the nation, and has made significant contributions to the nation through public service.

This paper is a slightly edited version of an article by Admiral Stockdale that first appeared in the May 1995 issue of *The World and I* magazine. It is reprinted here with the kind permission of News World Communications, Inc,

Albert C. Pierce

Albert C. Pierce
Director
Center for the Study of Professional Military Ethics
U.S. Naval Academy

Master of My Fate:
A Stoic Philosopher in a Hanoi Prison

When I debated Al Gore and Dan Quayle on television in October 1992, as candidates for vice president, I began my remarks with two questions that are perennially debated by every thinking human being: Who am I? Why am I here? The questions were relevant in terms of the evening's purpose, which was to introduce myself and let the American people know where I was coming from. But I also chose them for their broader relevance to my life: I am a philosopher.

I came to the philosophic life as a 38-year-old Navy pilot in graduate school at Stanford University. I had been in the Navy for 20 years and scarcely ever out of a cockpit. In 1962, I began my second year of studying international relations so I could become a strategic planner in the Pentagon. But my heart wasn't in it. Then I cruised into Stanford's philosophy corner one winter morning and met Philip Rhinelander, dean of humanities and sciences, who taught Philosophy 6, "The Problems of Good and Evil." Within 15 minutes, we had agreed that I would enter his two-term course in the middle. To makeup for my lack of background, I would meet him for an hour a week for a private tutorial in the study of his campus home.

Phil Rhinelander opened my eyes. In that study, it all happened for me—my inspiration, my dedication to the philosophic life. From then on, I was out of international relations and into philosophy. We went from Job to Socrates to Aristotle to Descartes. And then onto Kant, Hume, Dostoevsky, Camus. On my last session, he reached high on his wall of books and brought down a copy of the *Enchiridion*. He said, "I think you'll be interested in this."

Epictetus and the *Enchiridion*

Enchiridion means "ready at hand." In other words, it is a handbook. Its author, Epictetus, was a very unusual man of intelligence and sensitivity who gleaned wisdom rather than bitterness from his early first-hand exposure to extreme cruelty, the abuse of power, and self-indulgent debauchery.

Epictetus was born a slave around 50 AD. At 15 he was sold at a slave auction in Rome to Epaphroditus, a secretary to Emperor Nero. When Epaphroditus helped Nero complete his suicide attempt, Epictetus was able to venture out on his own. (Editor's Note: For a detailed description of Epictetus's background, see *Stockdale on Stoicism I: The Stoic Warriors Triad*, Occasional Paper Number One in this series.)

Being a serious and doubtless disgusted young man, he gravitated to the high-minded public lectures of the Stoic teachers who were then the philosophers of Rome. Epictetus eventually became apprenticed to the very best Stoic in the empire, Musonius Rufus. After ten or more years of study, he achieved the status of philosopher in his own right. With that came true freedom, and the preciousness of that was duly celebrated by the former slave. In his works, individual freedom is praised about seven times more frequently than it is in the New Testament. The Stoics held that all human beings were equal in the eyes of God: male and female, black and white, slave and free.

Epictetus speaks like a modern person, using "living speech," not the literary Attic Greek we are used to in men of that tongue. The *Enchiridion* was actually penned not by Epictetus, who was above all else a determined teacher and man of modesty who would never take the time to transcribe his own lectures, but by one of his most meticulous and determined students, Arrian, who, with Epictetus's consent, took down his words verbatim. Arrian bound the lectures into books; in the two years that he was enrolled in Epictetus's school, he filled eight books. Arrian put the *Enchiridion* together as highlighted extractions "for the busy man." That last morning, Rhinelander told me, "As a military man, I think you'll have special interest in this. Frederick the Great never went on a campaign without a copy of this handbook in his kit."

Stoicism is a noble philosophy that has proven to be more practicable than a modern cynic would expect. The Stoic viewpoint is often misunderstood because the casual reader misses the point—that all talk is in reference to the "inner life." Stoics belittle physical harm, but this is not braggadocio. They are speaking of it in comparison to the devastating agony of shame they fancied good men generating when they knew in their hearts that they had failed to do their duty *vis-a-vis* their fellow men or God. Though pagan, the Stoics had a monotheistic natural religion and were great contributors to Christian thought. The fatherhood of god and the brotherhood of man were Stoic concepts prior to Christianity. In fact, Chrysippus, one of their early theoreticians, made the analogy of what might be called the soul of the universe to the breath of a human *(pneuma,* in Greek). Saint Paul, a Hellenized Jew brought up in Tarsus, a Stoic town in Asia Minor, always used the Greek word *pneuma,* or breath, for soul.

The Stoic demand for disciplined thought naturally won only a small minority to its standard, but those few were the strongest characters of that time. In theory a doctrine of pitiless perfectionism, Stoicism actually created men of courage, saintliness, and goodwill. Rhinelander singled out three examples: Cato the Younger, Emperor Marcus Aurelius, and Epictetus. Cato was the great Roman Republican who pitted himself against Julius Caesar. He was the unmistakable hero of our own George Washington; scholars find quotations of Cato in Washington's Farewell Address—without quotation marks. Emperor Marcus Aurelius took the Roman Empire to the pinnacle of its power and influence. And Epictetus, the great teacher, played his part in changing the leadership of Rome from the swill he had known under Nero to the power and decency it knew under Marcus Aurelius.

Epictetus drew the same sort of audience Socrates had drawn 500 years earlier—young aristocrats destined for careers in finance, the arts, public service. The best families sent him their sons in their middle 20s—to be told what the good life consisted of, to be disabused of the idea that they deserved to become playboys, and to be taught that their job was to serve their fellow men.

Epictetus explained that his curriculum was not about "revenues or income, or peace or war, but about happiness and unhappiness, success and failure, slavery and freedom." His model graduate was not a person "able to speak fluently about philosophic principles as an idle babbler, but about things that will do you good if your child dies, or your brother dies, or if you must die or be tortured. . . . Let others practice lawsuits, others study problems, others syllogisms; here you practice how to die, how to be enchained, how to be racked, how to be exiled." A man is responsible for his own "judgments, even in dreams, in drunkenness, and in melancholy madness." Each individual brings about his own good and his own evil, his good fortune, his ill fortune, his happiness, and his wretchedness. It is unthinkable that one man's error could cause another's suffering; suffering, like everything else in Stoicism, was all internal—remorse at destroying yourself.

Epictetus was telling his students that there can be no such thing as being the "victim" of another. You can only be a "victim"of yourself. It's all in how you discipline your mind. Who is your master? "He who has authority over any of the things on which you have set your heart. . . . What is the result at which all virtue aims? Serenity. . . . Show me a man who though sick is happy, who though in danger is happy, who though in prison is happy, and I'll show you a Stoic."

Fighter Squadron Commander

When I got my degree, Sybil and I packed up our four sons and family belongings and headed to Southern California. Our new home was to be in Coronado. I was to take command of fighter squadron 51, flying supersonic F-8 Crusaders, at Miramar and at sea aboard carriers. Exactly three years after we drove out of our driveway in Los Altos Hills, I was shot down and captured.

I was not a book worm throughout those three years before I was shot down; most of the time I was busy at sea in the western Pacific. I launched on three seven-month cruises, all centered on the buildup and explosions of the Southeast Asian war. I was in command throughout, the last cruise as the commander of the air wing on the *Oriskany*. I dropped the first bombs of the war into North Vietnam and flew more than 100 missions in the flak.

But I was a changed and better man for my introduction to philosophy, and especially to Epictetus. I was on a different track—certainly not an anti-military track, but to some extent an anti-organization track. Against the backdrop of all the posturing and fumbling that peacetime military organizations seem to have to go through, to accept the need for graceful and unselfconscious improvisation under pressure, to break away from set procedures, forces you to be reflective as you put a new mode of operation together. I had become a man detached—not aloof but detached— able to throw out the book without the slightest hesitation when it no longer matched the external circumstances. I was able to put juniors over seniors without embarrassment when their wartime instincts were more reliable. This new abandon, this new built-in flexibility I had gained, was to pay off later in prison.

My bedside table on the ship was stacked not with busy-work to impress my boss, but with Stoic readings: the *Discourses,* Xenophon's *Memorabilia,* recollections of Socrates, and of course, *The Iliad* and *The Odyssey.* Epictetus expected his students to be familiar with Homer's plots.

The Stoics were the ultimate warriors. The Roman Stoics coined the formula, *Vivere Militare!*—Life is being a soldier. Epictetus said in *Discourses:* "Do you not know that life is a soldier's service? One must keep guard, another go out to reconnoiter, another take the field. If you neglect your responsibilities when some severe order is laid upon you, do you not understand to what a pitiful state you bring the army in so far as in you lies?"*Enchiridion:*

> Remember, you are an actor in a drama of such sort as the Author chooses—if short, then in a short one; if long, then in a long one. If it be his pleasure that you should enact a poor man, or a cripple, or a ruler, see that you act it well. For this is your business—to act well the given part, but to choose it belongs to Another. . . . Every one of us, slave or free, has come into this world with innate conceptions as to good and bad, noble and shameful, becoming and unbecoming,

happiness and unhappiness, fitting and inappropriate. . . . If you regard yourself as a man and as a part of
some whole, it is fitting for you now to be sick and now
to make a voyage and run risks, and not to be in want,
and on occasion to die before your time. Why, then, are
you vexed? Would you have someone else be sick of a
fever now, someone else go on a voyage, someone else
die? For it is impossible in such a body as ours, that is,
in this universe that envelopes us, among these fellow
creatures of ours, that such things should not happen,
some to one man, some to another.

Becoming a Prisoner

On September 9, 1965, I flew at 500 knots right into a flak
trap, at treetop level, in a little A-4 airplane that I suddenly couldn't
steer because it was on fire, its control system shot out. After ejection, I had about 30 seconds to make my last statement in freedom
before I landed in the main street of a little village right ahead.
And, so help me, I whispered to myself: "Five years down there, at
least. I'm leaving the world of technology and entering the world
of Epictetus."

"Ready at hand" from the *Enchiridion* as I ejected from that
airplane was the understanding that a Stoic always kept separate files
in his mind for those things that are "up to him" and those things
that are "not up to him." Another way of saying it is those things
which are "within his power" and those things which are "beyond
his power." Up to me, within my power, within my will, are my
opinions, my aims, my aversions, my own grief, my own joy, my
attitude about what is going on, my own good, and my own evil.

To explain why "your own good and your own evil" is on that
list, I quote Alexander Solzhenitsyn's *Gulag Archipelago:* "Gradually
it was disclosed to me that the line separating good and evil passes

not between states nor between classes nor between political parties, but right through every human heart." Long before reading Solzhenitsyn, I learned that good and evil are not abstractions—the only good and evil that mean anything are right in your own heart.

But a greater realization is that of your own fragility; that you could be reduced as I was from leading over 100 pilots and 1,000 men to "taking the ropes" in a matter of minutes. This is an example of not having control over your station in life. (Editor's Note: For a more in-depth discussion of good and evil and things within our power, see *Stockdale on Stoicism I: The Stoic Warrior's Triad*, Occasional Paper Number One in this series.)

Everybody does have to play the game of life. You can't just walk around saying, "I don't give a damn about health, or wealth, or whether I'm sent to prison or not." Epictetus says everybody should play the game of life—that the best play it with "skill, form, speed, and grace." But like most games, you play it with a ball. Your team devotes all its energies to getting the ball across the line. But after the game, what do you do with the ball? Nobody much cares. It's not worth anything. The competition, the game, was the thing. The ball was "used" to make the game possible, but it in itself is not of any value that would justify falling on your sword for it.

The ball-game analogy, incidentally, is almost a verbatim quote of Epictetus's explanation to his students in Nicoipolis, colonial Greece, 2,000 years ago.

My Mission in Prison

So I took those core thoughts into prison; I also remembered a lot of attitude-shaping remarks. Here's Epictetus on how to stay off the hook: "A man's master is he who is able to confer or remove whatever that man seeks or shuns. Whoever then would be free, let him wish nothing, let him decline nothing, which depends on others; else he must necessarily be slave." And here's why never to beg: "For it is better to die of hunger, exempt from fear and guilt, than to live in affluence and with perturbation." Begging sets up a demand for *quid pro quo*, deals, agreements, reprisals—the pits.

If you want to protect yourself from "fear and guilt"—and those are the crucial pincers, the real long-term destroyers of will—you have to get rid of all your instincts to compromise, to meet people halfway. You have to learn to stand aloof, never give openings for deals, never level with your adversaries. You have to become what Ivan Denisovich called a "slow movin' cagey prisoner."

All that, over the previous three years, I had unknowingly put away for the future. So when bailing out of my A-4, after the gang tackling and pummeling was over (it lasted for two or three minutes before a man with a pith helmet got there to blow his police whistle), I had a very badly broken leg that I felt sure would be with me for life. My hunch turned out to be right. Later, I felt some relief—but only minor—from another admonition of Epictetus that I remembered: "Lameness is an impediment to the leg, but not to the Will; and say this to yourself with regard to everything that happens. For you will find such things to be an impediment to something else, but not truly to yourself."

So in prison I had become a man with a mission. To explain this, let me unload a little emotional baggage that was part of my military generation's legacy in 1965.

In the aftermath of the Korean War, just over 10 years before, we all had memories of reading about and seeing early television news accounts of U.S. government investigations into the behavior of some American prisoners of war in North Korea and mainland China. The gist of it was that in prison camps for Americans, it was every man for himself. Since those days, I've come to know officers who were prisoners of war there, and I now see much of that as selective reporting and as a bum rap. However, there were cases of young soldiers who were confused by the times, scared to death, in cold weather, treating each other like dogs fighting over scraps, throwing each other out in the snow to die, and nobody doing anything about it.

This could not go on, and President Eisenhower commissioned the writing of the American Fighting Man's Code of Conduct. It was written in the form of a personal pledge. Article 4:

> If I become a prisoner of war, I will keep faith with my fellow prisoners. I will give no information or take part in any action which might be harmful to my comrades. If I am senior, I will take command. If not, I will obey the lawful orders of those appointed over me and will back them up in every way.

In other words, as of the moment Eisenhower signed that document, American prisoners of war were never to escape the chain of command; the war goes on behind bars.

As an insider, I knew the whole setup; that the North Vietnamese already held about 25 prisoners, probably in Hanoi, and as I was the only wing commander to survive an ejection, that I would be their senior, their commanding officer—and would remain so, very likely, throughout this war that I felt sure would last at least another five years. And here I was, starting off crippled and flat on my back.

Epictetus turned out to be right. All told, it was only a temporary setback from things that were important to me, and being cast in the role as the sovereign head of an American expatriate colony which was destined to remain autonomous, out of communication with Washington, for years on end, was very important to me. I was determined to "play well the given part."

The key word for all of us at first was fragility. Each of us, before we were ever in shouting distance of another American, was made to "take the ropes." That was a real shock to our systems—and as with all shocks, its impact on our inner selves was a lot more impressive and lasting and important than to our limbs and torsos. These were the sessions where we were taken down to submission and made to blurt out distasteful confessions of guilt and American complicity into antique tape recorders, and then to be put in what I call "cold soak," six or eight weeks of total isolation to "contemplate our crimes." What we actually contemplated was what even the most self-satisfied American saw as his betrayal of himself and everything he stood for. It was there that I learned what "Stoic harm" meant. A shoulder broken, a bone in my back broken, and a leg broken twice were peanuts by comparison. Epictetus said: "Look not for any greater harm than this: destroying the trustworthy, self-respecting, well-behaved man within you."

When put into a regular cell block, hardly an American came out of that without responding something like this when first whispered to by a fellow prisoner next door: "You don't want to talk to me; I am a traitor." And because we were equally fragile, it seemed to catch on that we all replied something like this: "Listen, pal, there are no virgins in here. You should have heard the kind of statement I made. Snap out of it. We're all in this together. What's your name? Tell me about yourself." To hear that last was, for most new prisoners just out of initial shake-down and cold soak, a turning point in their lives.

A Society of Prisoners

We organized a clandestine society via our wall tap code—a society with our own laws, traditions, customs, even heroes. To explain how it could be that we would order each other into more torture, order each other to refuse to comply with specific demands, intentionally call the bluff of our jailers and force them to repeat the process described above, I'll explain with an apocryphal statement that could have come from at least half of those wonderful, competitive fly-boys I found myself locked up with:

> We are in a spot like we've never been in before. But we deserve to maintain our self-respect, to have the feeling we are fighting back. We can't refuse to do every degrading thing they demand of us, but it's up to you, boss, to pick out things we must all refuse to do, unless and until they put us through the ropes again. We deserve to sleep at night. We at least deserve to have the satisfaction that we are hewing to our leader's orders. Give us the list: What are we to take torture for?

This was a first step in claiming what was rightfully ours. Epictetus said: "The judge will do some things to you which are thought to be terrifying; but how can he stop you from taking the punishment he threatened?" That's my kind of Stoicism. You have a right to make them hurt you, and they don't like to do it. The prison commissar told my fellow prisoner Ev Alvarez when he was released: "You Americans were nothing like the French; we could count on them to be reasonable."

I put a lot of thought into what my first orders should be. They would be orders that could be obeyed, not a "cover your ass" move of reiterating some U.S. government policy like "name, rank, serial number and date of birth," which had no chance of standing up in the torture room. My mind-set was, "We here under the gun are the experts, we are the masters of our fate. Ignore guilt-inducing echoes of hollow edicts, throw out the book, and write your own." My orders came out as easy-to-remember acronyms. The principal one was BACK US. Don't **B**ow in public; stay off the **A**ir; admit no **C**rimes; never **K**iss them good-bye. **US** could be interpreted as United States, but really meant that each of us had to work at the lowest common denominator, never negotiating for himself but only for all.

Prison life became a crazy mixture of an old regime and a new one. The old was the political prison routine mainly for dissenters and domestic enemies of the state. It was designed and run by old-fashioned Third-World Communists of the Ho Chi Minh cut. It revolved around the idea of "repentance" for "crimes" of anti-social behavior. American prisoners, street criminals, and domestic political enemies of the state were all in the same prison. We never saw a "POW camp" like in the movies. The Communist jail was part psychiatric clinic and part reform school. North Vietnamese protocol called for making all their inmates demonstrate shame, bowing to all guards, heads low, never looking at the sky. It meant frequent sessions with your interrogator, if for no other reason than to check your attitude. And if judged "wrong," then you were maybe down the torture chute of confession of guilt, of apology, and then the inevitable payoff—the atonement.

The new regime, superimposed on the above, was for Americans only. It was a propaganda factory, supervised by young, English-speaking, bureaucratic army officers with quotas to fill, quotas set by the political arm of the government: press interviews with visiting left-wing Americans, propaganda films to shoot (starring intimidated people they called "American Air Pirates"), and so on.

An encapsulated history of how this bifurcated prison philosophy fared is this: The propaganda footage and interviews started to backfire. Smart American college men were salting their acts with double-meaninged sentences, gestures read as funny-obscene by Western audiences, and practical jokes. One of my best friends,

82

tortured to give names of pilots he knew who had turned in their wings in opposition to the war, said there were only two: Lieutenants Clark Kent and Ben Casey. That went on the front page of the *San Diego Union*, and somebody sent a copy back to the government in Hanoi. As a result of that friendly gesture from a fellow American, Nels Tanner went into three successive days of rope torture, followed by 123 days in leg stocks—all while isolated, of course.

So after several of these stunts, which cost the Vietnamese much loss of face, North Vietnam resorted to getting its propaganda from only the relatively few Americans they could trust not to act up—real loners who, for different reasons, never joined the prisoner organization, never wanted to get into the tap-code network, well-known sleaze balls we came to call "finks."

The great mass of the other Americans in Hanoi were, by all standards, "honorable prisoners," but that is not to say that there was anything like a homogeneous prison regime we all shared. People like to think that because we were all in the Hanoi prison system, we had all these common experiences. It's not so. These differing regimes became marked when our prison organization stultified the propaganda efforts of this two-headed monster called the "Prison Authority." The North Vietnamese turned to vengeance against the leadership of my organization and to an effort to break down the morale of the others baiting them with an amnesty program in which they would compete for early release by being compliant to North Vietnam's wishes.

To the "Dark Place"

In May 1967, the PA system blared out: "Those of you who repent, truly repent, will be able to go home before the war is over. Those few diehards who insist on inciting the other criminals to oppose the camp authority will be sent to a special dark place." I immediately put out an order forbidding any Americans to accept early release, but that is not to say I was a lone man on a white horse. My order was accepted with obvious relief and spontaneous jubilation by the overwhelming majority.

Guess who went to the dark place. They isolated my leadership team—myself and my ten top cohorts—and sent us into exile. The Vietnamese worked very hard to learn our habits, and they knew who were the troublemakers and who were not making any waves. They isolated those I trusted most: those with a long record of solitary and rope-mark pedigrees. Not all were seniors. One of my 10 was only 24 years old—born after I was in the Navy. He was a product of my recent shipboard tendencies: "When instincts and rank are out of phase, take the guy with the instincts." All of us stayed in solitary throughout, starting with two years in leg irons in a little high-security prison right beside North Vietnam's "Pentagon"— their Ministry of Defense, a typical, old French building.

There are chapters upon chapters after that, but what they came down to in my case was a strung-out vengeance fight between the Prison Authority and those of us who refused to quit trying to be our brothers' keepers. The stakes grew to nervous-breakdown proportions. One of the 11 of us died in that little prison we called Alcatraz. There was not a man who wound up with less than three and a half years of solitary, and four of us had more than four years.

Howie Rutledge, one of the four of us with more than four years, went back to school and got a master's degree after we got home. His thesis concentrated on the question of whether long-term erosion of human purpose was more effectively achieved by torture or isolation. He mailed out questionnaires to us (who had also taken the ropes at least 10 times), and others with records of extreme prison abuse. He found that those who had less than two years' isolation and plenty of torture said torture was the trump card; those with more than two years' isolation and plenty of torture said that, for long-term modification of behavior, isolation was the way to go. From my viewpoint, you can get used to repeated rope torture—there are some tricks for minimizing your losses in that game. But keep a man, even a very strong-willed man, in isolation for three or more years, and he starts looking for a friend, any friend, regardless of nationality or ideology.

Epictetus once gave a lecture to his faculty complaining about the common tendency of new teachers to slight the stark realism of Stoicism's challenges in favor of giving the students an uplifting, rosy picture of how they could meet the harsh requirements of the good life painlessly. Epictetus said: "Men, the lecture-room of the philosopher is a hospital; students ought not to walk out of it in pleasure, but in pain." If Epictetus's lecture room was a hospital, my prison was a laboratory—a laboratory of human behavior. I chose to test his postulates against the demanding real-life challenges of my laboratory.

I'm not talking about brainwashing; there is no such thing. I'm talking about having looked over the brink, and seen the bottom of the pit, and realizing the truth of that linchpin of Stoic thought: that the thing that brings down a man is not pain but shame!

Why did those men in "cold soak" after their first rope trip eat their hearts out and feel so unworthy when the first American contacted them? Epictetus knew human nature well. In that prison laboratory, I know of not a single case where a man was able to erase his pangs of conscience with some laid-back, pop-psychology theory of cause and effect. Epictetus emphasizes time and again the fact that a man who lays the causes of his actions on to third parties or forces is not leveling with himself. He must live with his own judgments if he is to be honest with himself." But if a person subjects me to fear of death, he compels me," says a student. "No," says Epictetus, "It is neither death, nor exile, nor toil, nor any such things that is the cause of your doing, or not doing, anything, but only your opinions and the decisions of your Will."

"What is the fruit of your doctrines?" someone asked Epictetus. "Tranquility, fearlessness, and freedom," he answered. You can have these only if you are honest and take responsibility for your own actions. You've got to get it straight! You are in charge of you.

In prison, I never tapped or mentioned Stoicism once. You soon learned that if the guy next door was doing okay, that meant that he had all his philosophical ducks lined up in his own way. But some sharp guys read the signs in my actions. After one of my long isolations outside the cell-blocks of the prison, I was brought back into signaling range of the fold. My point of contact was a man named Dave Hatcher. As was standard operating procedure on a first contact after a long separation, we started off not with gushes of news but with, first, an agreed-upon danger signal; second, a cover story for each of us if we were caught; and third, a back-up communications system if this link was compromised—"slow movin' cagey prisoner" precautions. Hatcher's back-up system for me was a notedrop by an old sink near a place we called the Mint, the isolation cell-block of his wing of the prison—a place he rightly guessed I would soon enough be in. Every day we would signal for 15 minutes, over a wall between his cell-block and my "no-man's-land."

Try to Check Out

Then I got back into trouble. At that time, the commissar of prisons had had me isolated and under almost constant surveillance for the year since I had staged a riot in Alcatraz to get us out of leg irons. I was barred from all prisoner cell-blocks. I had special handlers, and they caught me with an outbound note that gave leads

I knew the interrogators could develop through torture. The result would be to implicate my friends in "black activities," as the North Vietnamese called them. I had been through those ropes more than a dozen times, and I knew I could contain material—so long as they didn't know I knew it. But this note would open doors that could lead to more people getting killed in there. We had lost a few in big purges—I think in torture overshoots—and I was getting tired of it.

It was the fall of 1969. I had been in this role for four years, and saw nothing left for me to do but check out. I was solo in the main torture room in an isolated part of the prison the night before what they told me would be my day to spill my guts. There was an eerie mood in the prison. Ho Chi Minh had just died and special dirge music was in the air. I was to sit up all night in traveling irons. My chair was near the only pane-glass window in the prison. I was able to waddle over and break the window stealthily. I went after my wrist arteries with the big shards. I had knocked the light out, but the patrol guard happened to find me passed out in a pool of blood but still breathing. The Vietnamese went to General Quarters, got their doctor, and saved me.

Why? It was not until after I was released years later that I learned that that very week, my wife, Sybil, was in Paris demanding humane treatment for prisoners. She was on world news, a public figure, and the last thing the North Vietnamese needed was me dead. There was a very solemn crowd of senior North Vietnamese officers in that room as I was revived. Prison torture, as we had known it in Hanoi, ended for everybody that night.

Of course, it was months before we could be sure that was so. All I knew at the time was that, in the morning, after my arms had been dressed and bandaged, the commissar himself brought in a hot cup of sweet tea, told my surveillance guard to take off my leg irons, and asked me to sit at the table with him." Why did you do this, Sto-dale? You know I sit with the army's General Staff; they've asked for a full report this morning." (It was not unusual for us to talk like that by that time.) But he never once mentioned the note, nor did anybody else thereafter. That was unprecedented. After a couple of months in a tiny isolated cell we called Calcutta to let my arms heal, they blindfolded me and walked me right into the "Las Vegas" cell block. The isolation and special surveillance were over. I was put, solo of course, in the Mint.

Dave Hatcher knew I was back because I walked under his window, and though he could not peek out, he could listen, and over the years he had attuned his ear to my walking "signature," my limping gait. Soon enough, the rusty wire over the sink in the washroom was bent to the north—Dave Hatcher's signal for "note in the bottle under the sink for Stockdale." Like an old fighter pilot, I checked my six o'clock, scooped the note up fast, and concealed it in my prison pajama pants, carefully. Back in my cell, after the guard locked the door, I sat on my toilet bucket—where I could stealthily jettison the note if the peephole cover moved—and unfolded Hatcher's sheet of low-grade paper toweling on which he had printed with rat dropping, without comment or signature, the last verse of Ernest Henley's poem *Invictus:*

It matters not how strait the gate,
How charged with punishment the scroll,
I am the master of my fate:
I am the captain of my soul.

Reflection

"A man's character is his fate."

—HERACLITUS

Some believe that we are born with a preordained destiny and nothing we do can alter this.

I disagree with this sentiment. I believe that our personalities, initiative, work ethic, and most importantly, our character, shape the direction and outcomes of our lives, and therefore, our destiny.

My life's experience has led me to believe that even though we are all are gifted at birth with widely varying levels of intelligence, aptitude and specific talents, those who perform best and achieve more in life are not always those born with the most natural gifts.

I believe that the path people take in life and where that path leads them depends largely on a single factor: their character. Said another way, I feel that no number of opportunities granted, riches gained and other forms of recognition received can alter the fact that a person is lacking in character, and my experience has been that such a person will inevitably fail or be shamed by his or her own behavior.

On the other hand, no amount of hardship, obstacles and setbacks can truly defeat a person whose core being is built upon a foundation of sound character.

Character > Fate

"The Spartans do not ask how many the enemy are, but where they are."

—AGIS II

Throughout my life, whenever I began to pursue lofty goals or difficult challenges , there were always naysayers who essentially told me that my objectives were either unrealistic, or that they felt that I did not possess the aptitude or ability to achieve them.

In hindsight, most of the naysayers were timid souls who'd settled for the comfort and safety that resides in being mediocre. They dared not try truly difficult things, lest they fail for all to see, yet they never hesitated to criticize those who were courageous enough to step outside of their comfort zones in the pursuit of personal and professional growth.

I learned to quickly identify the naysayers and avoid them, lest their defeatist attitudes infect my mind, and to surround myself with like-minded, optimistic people who shared my insatiable thirst for things that challenged me and pushed me to the edge of my limitations, real or perceived.

Taking heed of the sentiment of this Spartan's quote, I've learned to say to myself, "Why not me, and why not now?"

"The key is to keep company only with people who uplift you, whose presence calls forth your best."

—EPICTETUS

I've learned through experience that the people we allow into our inner circle do one of two things, they either add energy, positivity and other forms of value to my personal development, or they drain energy, inject negativity and become obstacles to my growth as a man.

Surrounding myself with people who become role models, mentors and sources of inspiration and advice has been essential to making progress on my lifelong quest for personal excellence.

As important to the success of this quest was the realization that people who bring forth negativity and defeatist attitudes must be identified as early as possible and be kept at a distance.

We tend to become like those we closely associate with, and thus, relative to our own development and maximization of our growth potential, we should ensure that we seek to be close to only those who are better than us in various ways.

"A gem cannot be polished without friction,
nor a man perfected without trials."

—Seneca

Human nature steers us to seek the path of least resistance in our daily lives, personally and professionally. In prehistoric times, this genetic instinct had evolved in humans so they could conserve energy in an environment in which food was scarce and the need for sudden bursts of life-saving activity was pervasive.

As a young athlete, I observed that the very best competitors in my chosen sport of wrestling were those who'd spent years seeking the very best competition, and who'd made a habit out of competing against and training with wrestlers who were superior to them from a technical, physical and experience perspective.

Likewise, as a young, enlisted Marine, I observed that even within units full of hardened combat veterans from World War II, the Korean War, and the Vietnam conflict, there were individuals who had reputations for being truly exceptional Marines. In almost every instance, I observed that these Marines were very demanding of themselves and had established personal and professional standards of excellence that required them to work hard on a daily basis to satisfy.

The common denominator among the wrestlers and Marines I'd observed was their relentless drive to achieve excellence and their willingness to commit to doing whatever it took to achieve it. More importantly, these high-achievers did not sit around and wait for opportunities to get better to magically appear in front of them, they sought them out and did whatever necessary to insert themselves in environments in which they could learn and grow.

The main lesson I learned from my observations was that if I continued to "do hard things" there was a high probability that good things would happen for me!

"Until we have begun to go without them,
we fail to realize how unnecessary many things are.
We've been using them not because
we needed them, but because
we had them."

—SENECA

As a young, enlisted Marine, I often spent my hard-earned money on things that I desired more for their image than for their substance or utility. Some of this was due to the newness of actually having a steady income for the first time in my life; I found it somewhat exhilarating to be able to afford things that just a couple of years prior were simply unattainable from a financial perspective.

Over time, I observed that many of the people I admired, most of whom were quite successful financially, seemed to place little value on the acquisition of things simply for the sake of acquiring them. Instead they seemed to be satisfied with driving a car that was several years old, or living in the modest homes that they moved into many years ago when they weren't earning much money.

I began to follow their example and ask myself if something I was considering buying was really necessary, or perhaps something I felt would simply be nice to have, and perhaps even impress others when they saw that I'd acquired it.

I learned to ask myself, "Will this help me achieve my goals or otherwise improve my life on a prolonged basis, or will I soon tire of it and place it in a closet where it will sit unused?"

When I decided to pass on buying what it was that had captured my fancy, more often than not, I soon realized that I really didn't need it. And this has led me to reflexively and continuously ask myself this question relative to all aspects of my life: "What do I really need?"

"If you are distressed by anything external, the pain is not due to the thing itself, but to your estimate of it; and this you have the power to revoke at any moment."

—MARCUS AURELIUS

Like most people, I have had experiences that caused me great emotional pain.

With the benefit of hindsight, I realize that while these experiences were hurtful in various ways, it was failure to control my emotions that greatly amplified and prolonged any pain I felt.

Over time, I learned that getting up and "dusting myself off" so to speak was the quickest way out of any hurt or negativity I was feeling.

"The happiness of your life depends
upon the quality of your thoughts."

—MARCUS AURELIUS

From the moment we awake each morning, our minds are busily processing our thoughts. Often, we are ruminating about things we can't control, and we yet don't even notice that we've allowed our minds to be consumed by these thoughts, which are typically negative in nature.

This great philosopher is telling is that when we allow our thoughts to be consumed by emotions or issues that don't help us on our path to virtue and excellence, we are making ourselves unhappy. The ancient Stoics constantly remind us that intelligently disciplined people remain in control of their thoughts and those thoughts are reflected in the choices they make, which lead to the direction their lives take.

I've learned that I am at my best when I slow down to think about what I am actually thinking about. This enables me to determine whether the thoughts that are dominating my mind are leading me toward positive or negative decisions and outcomes.

"They can conquer who believe they can."

—VIRGIL

With the benefit of hindsight, I now realize that all significant achievements in my life were preceded by my belief that I could succeed!

Often, my beliefs were deemed unrealistic by others, and this caused me to develop a sense of determination to stay the course I'd chosen to travel, and to "grow a thick skin" relative to the doubts, ridicule and negativity that may come from others.

Countless philosophers and highly accomplished people have made statements similar to that of Virgil's; they all are essentially saying that whether a person believes they can succeed or that they cannot, the outcomes they experience generally align with their beliefs.

Bottom Line: To achieve something, you must truly believe that you can achieve it. Without this unshakeable belief in yourself, your chances of success are greatly diminished.

"Who then is invincible?
The one who cannot be upset by anything
outside their reasoned choice."

—EPICTETUS

This quote by Epictetus is easy to understand, but often difficult to do. But, as I've matured, I have learned (often the hard way!) that worrying about things that I cannot control or influence is an exercise in futility, and a waste of time that could be spent on thoughts that could lead to intelligent decisions and positive outcomes.

Regarding the ever-present criticisms and "sniping from the peanut gallery," I think the words of one the best visionaries and entrepreneurs in America's history are wise counsel to all:

> "Your time is limited, so don't waste it living someone else's life. Don't be trapped by dogma—which is living with the results of other people's thinking. Don't let the noise of other's opinions drown out your own inner voice. And most important, have the courage to follow your heart and intuition. They somehow already know what you truly want to become. Everything else is secondary." —Steve Jobs

> *"Freedom is the only worthy goal in life.*
> *It is won by disregarding things that lie*
> *beyond our control."*
>
> **—EPICTETUS**

One major theme that is emphasized in Stoicism is that people should remain focused on that which they can actually control or influence and avoid becoming consumed or distracted by that which they cannot.

Obviously, this is often easier said than done, and at times, I've allowed myself to dwell on issues and situations that I could not have an impact upon, and this enabled them to have a negative impact upon me.

Life has taught me that I am happiest when I follow this advice!

"Don't explain your philosophy. Embody it."

—**EPICTETUS**

Actions > Words

"Rule your mind or it will rule you."

—Horace

I think most people will admit that they often allow their minds to become consumed with their fears, emotions and the everyday stressors of life. They can become paralyzed by thinking about what *could* happen vice what really *is* happening.

Trust me when I say that I've been there, done that . . . in spades!

Over time, I've learned to force myself to mentally detach from the "worst case" scenarios that are beginning to dominate my thoughts, and remember that in the past, the worst-case outcomes I feared almost never happened.

One simple technique that has helped me do this is to simply sit or lay down in a quite area and focus on my breathing, inhaling and exhaling to a count of 4 seconds each. Doing this has a very real physical effect on my body's state of relaxation and focusing on the breathing intervals keeps my mind off of the issue that was stressing me.

I learned this technique from a friend who was a former Navy SEAL. He called it "4x4 Breathing," and said he'd learned it during his early SEAL training. He found it so effective that he continued the practice after he left the military and became immersed in a very high-stress profession in Corporate America.

I urge you to reflect upon this and other relaxation techniques the next time you find yourself overwhelmed or in a spiral of negative thoughts. Horace's advice remains valid to this day, "rule your mind, or it will rule you."

Easier said than done, but it is true that we have total control over our thoughts.

Logical Thoughts > Emotional Thoughts

"I have often regretted my speech, never my silence."

—Publilius Syrus

This has been my experience, for sure!
There have been times in my life that being silent or wait-ing a while to express my thoughts or opinions would have saved me from avoidable and unnecessary stress, friction, misunderstand-ings, hurt feelings and damaged relationships.

I wish I'd become more adept at the art of listening earlier in my life, as I now know that in most situations, listening to what others have to say is essential to resolving problems and making progress toward individual and team goals.

To clarify, I mean *truly listening* to hear what others are saying and being willing to change my mind based upon what they said, instead of listening to them only with the intent of replying to them immediately after they stopped speaking.

"Be tolerant with others and strict with yourself."

—MARCUS AURELIUS

I've learned two very valuable things during my life, often via some painful and costly lessons:

- My shortcomings, problems, and failures are always the consequences of choices I've made. It is futile to blame others or accept excuses that I may offer myself.

- People do and say things for reasons that are often unknown to me. If I take time to reflect upon their past and present experiences, I'm better equipped to serve as the friend and ally they deserve.

> *"The secret of happiness, you see,
> is not found in seeking more, but in developing
> the capacity to enjoy less."*
>
> **—SOCRATES**

This quote resonates with me because I became happier once I understood the importance of enjoying the little things in life, rather than relentlessly striving for the next achievement or success.

I'm a driven person, a highly competitive "Type-A Meat Eater" for sure. Since I was a young man, I have felt a need to maximize the use of my natural talent and to work hard on the things I wanted to achieve. There's never been a time in my adult life that I was not pursuing and attacking audacious personal and professional goals.

At some point recently, I realized that I could accomplish just about anything I attempted to do, and that I no longer had anything left to prove to myself and the people who loved me. I thought that perhaps it was time to relax a bit and enjoy life's journey a bit more.

I now revel in my ability to do as I please each day; to sit quietly in my home and read a book; to have very little external friction in my life, as I remain vigilant to avoid inflicting self-imposed friction upon myself.

Take time to enjoy what you already have, my friends.

Often, in this life, less is truly more!

*"Success tends to create pride and blindness
in the hearts of men, while suffering teaches them
to be patient and strong."*

—XENOPHON

As a young, enlisted Marine, I was often guilty of responding to my successes and good fortune with a sense of entitlement and arrogance fueled by my own hubris.

When I became a non-commissioned officer and assumed leadership roles, I began to fully understand the concept of teamwork. I realized that most of the significant achievements in my life were the result of the effort and support of others, and not entirely by my own merit.

Conversely, I had a tendency to blame my failures and setbacks on others. I wasn't mature enough to know that most of them were almost entirely my fault, and that pointing fingers at others was the habit of an insecure and weak-minded person.

Once I fully embraced the concept of total accountability for my decisions and actions, I began to grow as a man and prosper at an exponential rate.

I've had to face many challenges, failures and setback during my life, and without question, they greatly influenced who I am as a man.

Without question, the most difficult times in my life shaped who I am as a man.

These times were often not a good place to be, but they were always a good place to be from!

108

"Choose well."

—**HOMER**

My parents taught me that "all choices have consequences." Anne Frank wrote, "Our lives are fashioned by our choices. First we make our choices. Then our choices make us."

I've made many choices during my life that proved to be wise and more than I care to admit that fall into the "What was I thinking?" category!

With the benefit of hindsight, I can see that most of the wise choices were made intelligently and were guided by logical thinking. Conversely, most of the poor decisions I've made were often made in haste or were overly influenced by my emotions.

So much of the Stoic way of life is centered around one's ability to control one's thoughts, and nowhere is this more critical than while making important decisions.

If I've learned anything in life, it is this:

Logical Decisions > Emotional Decisions

"I don't need a friend who changes when I change and who nods when I nod; my shadow does that much better."

—PLUTARCH

I've been blessed with friends who were willing to challenge my opinions, decisions and actions.

Though it has not always been easy to listen to them, experience has taught me that they are almost always right when they offer constructive criticisms and advice.

True friends tell me what I need to hear, not what I'd prefer to hear!

"Watch a man in times of . . . adversity to
discover what kind of man he is; for then at last
words of truth are drawn from the depths
of his heart, and the mask is torn off . . ."

—LUCRETIUS

Adversity, stress, and pressure enables you to finally see the real substance of someone.

Difficult times do not build a person's character, they reveal it for all to see.

> *"No man ever steps in the same river twice,*
> *for it's not the same river and he's not the same man."*
>
> **—Heraclitus**

I've grown the most when I forced myself to step into new, often intimidating "rivers."

Doing so almost always requires me to confront self-imposed limitations and irrational fears and emotions.

It is said that "iron sharpens iron" and I know that I've experienced the most growth when I've actively sought to "hone the blade of my being!"

*"Be strong, saith my heart; I am a soldier;
I have seen worse sights than this."*

—Homer, The Odyssey"

Three things I've learned:

- Past difficulties provide a frame of reference for current situations, and the ability to think: "I've been through much worse, and I will get through this, too."

- Though I often fear that the worst-case scenario is going to happen, it almost never does.

- Decisive action is better applied to problems earlier than later.

"The art of being a slave is to rule one's master."

—DIOGENES OF SINOPE

I've learned to accept that certain things are harmful to my well-being, or cause significant fear, anxiety, and stress.

Left unchallenged, these things could essentially control my life.

Whenever I've taken action to confront, defeat or neutralize these things, I've become happier and healthier.

Life is about choices.

I choose to master that which could render me a slave.

*"We must remember that one man is
much the same as another, and that he is best
who is trained in the severest school."*

—THUCYDIDES

This quote has been on the walls of my home and office for decades.

It reminds me that I am capable of achieving things that often seem unattainable if I am willing to immerse myself in disciplined study and take deliberate actions.

Anything I have achieved, others can, too.

Anything others have achieved, so can I.

Self-discipline > Imposed discipline

"Anger is an acid that can do more harm to the vessel in which it is stored than to anything on which it is poured."

—SENECA

I'm human and am capable of feeling anger.

I've learned over time that being angry at someone or something has never had any positive effect on me, the other person, or anything else.

Rational Thought > Anger

"*Only the dead have seen the end of the war.*"

—PLATO

Sadly, mankind has never found a way to avoid war, and I think Plato's words will echo throughout eternity.

Likewise, most of us will inevitably experience varying degrees of fear, anxiety, stress, disappointment and failure throughout our entire lives.

An intelligent person acknowledges this as reality.

A wise person knows that how one deals with reality can actually produce positive outcomes from even the most difficult situations.

Resilience > Apathy

"It is not so much our friends' help that helps us, as the confident knowledge that they will help us."

—EPICURUS

I'm blessed with friends who love me enough to tell me things I don't want to hear, but that I need to hear.

I hope that I've been as helpful to them as they've been to me.

A Friend's Love > The World's Riches

"With the right attitude,
Self-imposed limitations vanish."

—ALEXANDER THE GREAT

Every significant achievement in my life was at some point associated with:

- Self-doubt.

- Fear of failure.

- Knowing the odds were stacked against my chances of success.

- Criticism, negative comments, and even ridicule from others.

When asked to provide a quote for my high school yearbook photo that would reflect my personality, I came up with this:

"If you take a chance, you have a chance."

Courage to Try > Fear of Failure

"If you want something good, get it from yourself."

—EPICTETUS

I'm happiest when . . .

- I take full accountability for my life's direction.
- I help others be happy by helping them achieve their goals.
- I'm with people who know that I love them unconditionally.
- I feel loved, respected, and appreciated.

All choices have consequences. I choose happiness!

> *"Before you heal someone, ask him if he's willing to give up the things that make him sick."*
>
> **—HIPPOCRATES**

Experience has taught me that stress, disappointment and sadness can largely be eliminated if I avoid certain people, situations, and actions.

Often, when I have finally decided to do this, my life improves so quickly that I wonder why I didn't take action sooner.

Happiness is a choice.

*"What lies in our power to do,
lies in our power not to do."*

—ARISTOTLE

Over the years, as my ability to control my thoughts and actions increased, so did success and happiness in my personal and professional lives.

Self-discipline is the greatest form of discipline!

*"The desire for safety stands against every
great and noble enterprise."*

—TACITUS

I like knowing that others think well of me and perhaps even admire me for some of my accomplishments.

The truth is my most notable accomplishments required me to intentionally leave the comfort of the known for the uncertainty of the unknown, and that was often quite intimidating, and sometimes, literally terrifying.

So, it is not accomplishments nor accolades that I am most proud of, it is the knowledge that when faced with situations like this, I was able to defeat my instinctive desire to remain safe and steady and take actions that led to success.

I'm still afraid of some things.

And I will defeat them, too.

Victories of the Mind > Surrendering to Safety

"Nothing, to my way of thinking, is a better proof of a well-ordered mind than a man's ability to stop just where he is and pass some time in his own company."

—SENECA

Though I always seek advice from others on important matters, I am ultimately solely responsible for my decisions.

To make wise decisions, I need to be alone with my thoughts and reflect upon the various options available to me.

Throughout my life, some of the most enlightening conversations I've had were with myself!

"The wildest colts make the best horses."

—PLUTARCH

As an 8th grade student, I was expelled from Catholic school and a priest told my parents that I was incorrigible and likely to end up in prison one day.

He was wrong.

Experience has taught me that many people possess personalities, talent and high levels of energy that, if properly guided, can help them become very productive in all aspects of life.

These people do best when they are exposed to a patient and loving mentor.

"While we are postponing, life speeds by."

—Seneca

Looking back, I've waited too long to do some things, thinking, "I'll do it later."

As I grow older, I've realized that there is no guarantee of having a later, and that for some, it never comes.

Taking Action > Hoping and Dreaming

"We must exercise ourselves in the things which bring happiness, since, if that be present, we have everything, and, if that be absent, all our actions are directed toward attaining it."

—EPICURUS

I've learned that doings things in an attempt to make others happy does not always result in happiness for them, or me.

When I do things to help others achieve their goals, more often than not, happiness abounds.

Thus, for me, the surest way to find happiness is to help others bring their goals to fruition.

"*Pleasure in the job puts perfection in the work.*"

—**ARISTOTLE**

I perform best when I wake up excited and eager to seize the new day.

Doing so means that I never experience the drudgery of work, instead I feel the satisfaction that comes from doing what I am passionate about.

"How long are you going to wait before you
demand the best for yourself?"

—Epictetus

I have high expectations of myself.

I've learned that through a willingness to sacrifice and the relentless application of initiative and hard work, these expectations can be met and in many instances, exceeded.

I am solely responsible for the direction of my life.

"Remember that to change your mind and to accept correction are free acts too. The action is yours, based on your own free will, your own decision— and your own mind"

—MARCUS AURELIUS

I've learned that aside from matters of character and integrity, it's acceptable to change my mind on any issue when it is the result of logical thought.

And, when I set my ego aside and became approachable to those who could help me correct my own flawed thinking and actions, my life was enriched in many ways.

"A house that has a library in it has a soul."

—PLATO

Every mistake I've made or can possibly make in my personal and professional lives was made previously by others.

All I have to do to avoid repeating their mistakes is to invest the time required to read their insights and advice.

Books are as vital to my mind as is oxygen!

Reading = Gateway to Wisdom

"It's unfortunate that this has happened.
No.
It's fortunate that this has happened and I've remained
unharmed by it—not shattered by the present or
frightened of the future. It could have happened
to anyone. But not everyone could have remained
unharmed by it."

—MARCUS AURELIUS

I've experienced disappointment and failure during my life.

I often allowed myself to dwell on the worst possible outcome of such situations and anxiously hope it didn't happen.

Fortunately, the worst possible outcome rarely happened, especially when I focused my thoughts and actions less on the problem at hand and more on moving forward with optimism and confidence.

"If you want to improve, be content to be thought foolish and stupid with regard to external things. Don't wish to be thought to know anything; and even if you appear to be somebody important to others, distrust yourself."

—EPICTETUS

This is one of the most important leadership lessons that I can share. In my opinion, long term and high-level success as a leader is greatly impacted by how soon one has what I call "The Leadership Epiphany."

This epiphany happens on the day when you finally realize and accept that:

- You don't have to be the smartest person in the room.
- You're not expected to have all of the answers.
- Saying "I don't know" and "What do you recommend?" are actually signs of strength, not weakness.
- You genuinely feel more pride and satisfaction in the success of your teammates than in your own achievements.

While aimed at business leaders, these insights are applicable to one's personal life.

"Take example from the wrestling-masters. Has the boy fallen down? Get up, again, they say; wrestle again until you have made yourself strong. That's the sort of attitude you should have . . . For both ruin and salvation have their source within you."

—EPICTETUS

I entered the sport of wrestling when I was in the 3rd grade, and I loved it from the very first practice session I attended.

I wasn't a naturally gifted athlete and I learned many lessons via the embarrassment and disappointment that came with losing every match I ever wrestled during my grammar school years.

Most importantly, I learned how to reach deep within myself and "get up again," and this determination and refusal to quit has served me well in every aspect of life.

Looking back, most of my growth as a man was gained through lessons learned while attempting things that challenged me greatly, and in some instances, humbled me without mercy.

"No man has the right to be an amateur in the matter of physical training. It is a shame for a man to grow old without seeing the beauty and strength of which his body is capable."

—SOCRATES

We are all just one annual physical or unplanned trip to the emergency room removed from learning something that will change our lives forever.

Realizing this, I am determined to do everything in my power to optimize and preserve the healthy body and mind that I've been blessed with.

I'm healthier when I'm happy, and happier when I'm healthy.

Investing in my health and fitness is the wisest investment of all!

"Hang on to your youthful enthusiasms—you'll be able to use them better when you're older."

—SENECA

I've been blessed with the "Optimism Gene."
Whenever I start thinking about new goals or challenging obstacles to take on, I am still capable of getting as excited as a little boy receiving a new bike for his birthday.

This trait has served me so well that I hope that I never grow up!

"Do not view anything as beneficial that causes you to break a promise, lose your self-respect, or hate anyone."

—MARCUS AURELIUS

Character must be the guide for one's thoughts and actions when faced with temptations, personal gain at the expense of others, or an easy way out of difficult situations.

"Now, while enthusiasm is still fresh, those with an active interest should progress to better things. In this mode of life, much that is worth studying awaits you."

—SENECA

I possess little natural talent at anything that others might judge me as being skilled at.

Whatever successes I've had, came from hard work and sacrifice, both guided by the study of those who were what I wanted to become.

We are surrounded by wisdom, and we only need to study it and apply it to our own lives.

> *"I have often wondered how it is that every man loves himself more than all the rest of men, but yet sets less value on his own opinions of himself than on the opinions of others."*
>
> **—Marcus Aurelius**

I have a normal desire for others to think well of me.

I've learned that no matter what I do or how hard I try, there will always be some who simply do not have a high opinion of me.

When this happens, I engage in brutally honest reflection to determine if their opinions have merit, and if they do, I take action to improve myself.

In this way, even people who don't think well of me can help me become a better person.

> *"First learn the meaning of what you say,*
> *and then speak."*
>
> **—EPICTETUS**

Things I say can have an enduring positive or negative effect on a person.

I've learned that speaking with positive intent doesn't guarantee that my words will be viewed as such by another person.

Knowing that I only get one chance to say something for the first time, I try to do everything possible to ensure my words will be received as intended.

"Do not train a child to learn by force or harshness; but direct them to it by what amuses their minds, so that you may be better able to discover with accuracy the peculiar bent of the genius of each."

—Plato

I have four children.

Each of them is very different from the others, and none are "carbon copies" of me relative to their own visions of what happiness is, and how they want to spend their lives.

My role as a parent is to find out what they are passionate about and help them make their dreams come true.

This concept applies equally to each person that a leader is privileged to work with.

I wish I'd learned this much earlier than I did; I could have been much more effective as both parent and leader.

"How big is the little thing that was
given at the right time."

—MENANDER

Many of the most difficult times of my life were made more tolerable by the genuine love and encouragement of a friend. I try to be that friend to others, too, because everyone needs someone to be there for them when they're facing difficulties.

True Friends > The World's Riches

"Luck is when preparation meets opportunity."

—Seneca

At various points in my life, I've had the good luck to be exposed to exceptional people, environments and tribes associated with high-standards and the pursuit of excellence.

This, combined with initiative and hard work, enabled me to be prepared to perform well when some incredible opportunities came my way.

Luck may catapult a person into an arena, but once there, success comes via focused effort and relentless tenacity.

"If you really want to escape the things that harass you, what you're needing is not to be in a different place but to be a different person."

—SENECA

Learning to free myself from people, environments and situations that drain happiness from me has been one of the biggest lessons of my life.

At times, I've unwittingly allowed all three to negatively alter my thoughts and actions.

I've learned that my happiness is a like a garden that must be constantly tended to, lest the weeds overcome the beautiful flowers planted in it.

"When men speak ill of thee, live so as nobody may believe them."

—PLATO

As a young man, I'd get offended if I learned that someone had made negative comments about me that weren't true. I felt a need to defend my honor and reputation.

Over time, I realized that the best way to respond to unfair criticism is to simply continue to be myself and be confident that good people would take time to reflect upon the substance of my character and past behavior.

Resting on my past decisions, actions, and comments has proven to be the best defense against those who may speak ill of me.

"*People are like dirt. They can either nourish you and help you grow as a person or they can stunt your growth and make you wilt and die.*"

—PLATO

We were taught as children that we inevitably become like those we associate with, and we were cautioned to choose our friends wisely.

This is sound advice that never decreases in value during a person's life; it is as important to me now, at the age of 65, as it was when I was a young boy.

I believe that one's happiness and success in life is largely the result of whom one chooses to love, trust, associate with, and listen to.

As such, it is my responsibility to ensure that my "soil" is rich in nutrients, and to serve others by enriching their lives in the same way.

*"Educating the mind without educating the heart
is no education at all."*

—ARISTOTLE

Many educated people never rise above mediocrity because they lack the ability or desire to genuinely care about the needs of others.

These people are often rigid-minded and insist on doing the correct thing versus the right thing in any situation, and they never truly understand the difference between the former and the latter.

"Excellence is never an accident. It is always the result of high intention, sincere effort, and intelligent execution; it represents the wise choice of many alternatives—choice, not chance, determines your destiny."

—ARISTOTLE

I had superb role models when I was a young man. The common denominator among them was that their specific excellence and skills were the result of years of making wise choices combined with hard work.

Additionally, whenever a choice they'd made proved to be wrong (and they'd all been wrong at times) they did not blame others or curse their bad luck, they took decisive action to ensure they returned to the path of excellence.

Excellence is the result of intelligent choices fueled by focused relentlessness and tenacity.

*"Gratitude is not only the greatest of virtues,
but the parent of all the others."*

—Marcus Tullius Cicero

Doing things without expectations of anything in return is an admirable trait.

However, just because someone doesn't expect something does not mean he or she should not receive it.

Everyone needs to feel loved, respected and appreciated; they can only feel these emotions through kind words and actions given to them by others.

Words like the following do no good if left unspoken . . .

- I Love You
- I Trust You
- I Appreciate You
- I'm Blessed to Have You in My Life
- I Miss You

Say these things often to people who deserve them.
While you still can.

*"What I fear is not the enemy's strategy,
but our own mistakes."*

—THUCYDIDES

Success in war often comes from being able to rapidly exploit opportunities created by the enemy's mistakes.

This is true in most aspects of life.

Those who've gained wisdom from past mistakes accept that more will come, and that success lies in the ability to assess, decide, and act.

The wisest of all never make the same mistake twice.

"It is not because things are difficult that we do not dare; it is because we do not dare that things are difficult."

—SENECA

Fear of failure and embarrassment, if left unchecked, can prevent me from attempting things that leverage and enhance my best qualities.

At some point long ago, I realized that I actually found pleasure in trying things that I wasn't sure I could accomplish, and that others admired me for being willing to risk failure.

I also learned that because others almost always asked me to do things that they already knew that I could do, it was my responsibility to ensure that I faced a steady stream of audacious goals and difficult challenges.

As I reflect upon my life, it's obvious that most of my personal growth has happened by repeatedly entering the "Arena of Uncertainty."

"That which is used—develops.
That which is not used wastes away."

—HIPPOCRATES

One trait each of my early role models and mentors had in common was a relentless pursuit of self-improvement.

Knowing that such accomplished people were intentional life-long learners inspired me to become one, too.

I determined long ago that my approach to life was that I would rather "wear out" than "rust out."

"Follow where reason leads."

—ZENO OF CITIUM

L ife has taught me many lessons, and I wish I'd learned some much earlier than I did.

Among the most important:

- Character and integrity mean different things to different people, and I must remain true to my definitions of these traits.

- Trust is earned . . . every single day.

- Being respected for one's actions is more important than being respected for one's words.

- Rational thinking can be completely overwhelmed by emotion.

- I alone am responsible for my happiness and the direction of my life.

"*We're tight-fisted with property and money, yet think too little of wasting time, the one thing about which we should all be the toughest misers.*"

—SENECA

I'm amazed at how quickly the first 65 years of my life have come and gone.

I now view the time I have left as a precious gift that has an expiration date that I will never know.

I hope that date is far into the future, but I intentionally approach many aspects of my life as if it was tomorrow.

Today's actions > Dreams that run out of time

"All human actions have one or more of these seven causes: chance, nature, compulsions, habit, reason, passion, desire."

—ARISTOTLE

Aristotle's words are few, but are packed with wisdom, fuel for reflection and guidance for one's behavior.

Everything that I do is based upon one or more of the causes listed.

My experience has been that reason (rational thinking) produces the best outcomes.

"I judge you unfortunate because you have never lived through misfortune. You have passed through life without an opponent—no one can ever know what you are capable of, not even you."

—SENECA

Responding to life's trials and tribulations spurred me to change old habits, learn new things and develop the difficult to define traits of mental toughness and resilience.

I often felt pity for myself when I was confronted by defeat, disappointment or misfortune, but upon reflecting on what hard times did to bring out the very best in me, I realize how blessed I was to be repeatedly "thrown into fires" from which I could emerge a stronger person.

It's when I became confident enough to voluntarily throw myself into various types of fires that my growth as a man greatly accelerated.

"Employ your time in improving yourself by other men's writings, so that you shall gain easily what others have labored hard for."

—SOCRATES

The world has changed dramatically since the days of the ancient philosophers. I doubt they could have dreamed of what modern society, technology, etc., looks like.

However, in matters regarding human nature, their hard-won wisdom remains entirely relevant, because human beings are still driven by the same physical and emotional desires as their ancestors.

I have benefitted greatly from the counsel of men who lived thousands of years before I was born!

"If what you have seems insufficient to you, then though you possess the world, you will yet be miserable."

—SENECA

I've learned that there's a huge difference between striving for excellence and perfection.

Excellence, however distant and difficult is achievable through discipline and hard work.

Perfection is almost never achievable, yet I've observed people become consumed with chasing it, especially in their relationships with others.

Those who insist on perfection often overlook the good things and people in their lives, and they usually fail to find the former, and often lose the latter through neglect and indifference.

Be grateful for what you have, or you may wake up one day and realize it's gone!

"Those who are hardest to love need it the most."

—SOCRATES

Many of the very best people in our lives can be "hard to love" because of certain aspects of their personality and behavior.

I've learned that by being patient, I often discover one or more reasons why a person thinks, acts and talks as they do, and this enables me to better understand them.

Looking back at my own life, I realize that whenever I was the person who was "hard to love," special people were especially kind to me, and they helped me through whatever challenge I was facing at the moment.

Patience and kindness cost us nothing to give but are precious to the recipients.

"Is a world without pain possible?
Then don't ask the impossible."

—MARCUS AURELIUS

When training Marines in the art of knife fighting, a wise instructor will tell his students that they must enter such a fight with the acceptance of this fact: "Everyone gets cut in a knife fight."

This informs the student that the brutal reality of blade combat is that there will be blood, and some of it will be his own.

Fortunately, most of life's inevitable pain is not associated with physical injury, but it does occupy much of our thoughts at times.

I've learned not to dwell on the anticipation or fear of whatever pain life may bring me, but instead focus on strengthening my ability to deal with it.

"Excellence withers without an adversary."

—Seneca

As a young Marine, I was impressed by the fact that many older, highly accomplished Marines always seemed to be challenging themselves.

The self-discipline and quiet enthusiasm they displayed as they pushed themselves mentally and physically had a profound impact upon my outlook on life.

Over the years, I became skilled at some things as the result of adapting to some of the trials and tribulations life threw at me.

Without question, the most personal growth I've ever achieved was gained via the difficult challenges I sought on my own.

"*Any person capable of angering you becomes your master; he can anger you only when you permit yourself to be disturbed by him.*"

—ARISTOTLE

There have always been people who do not seek to deal with me honestly and with good intentions, but instead seem to enjoy saying or doing things sure to cause me to become angry.

These people add no value to my life; they have a draining effect on my happiness and productivity.

Experience has taught me that the sooner I distance myself from them, the better.

"Health is the soul that animates all the enjoyments of life, which fade and are tasteless without it."

—SENECA

M any people abandon their health while chasing career ambitions and wealth.

Sadly, when they finally acquire them, many people are not able to fully enjoy either due to health limitations brought on by years of neglect.

Investing in One's Health = Wisest Investment Possible

"We are too much accustomed to attribute to a single cause that which is the product of several, and the majority of our controversies come from that."

—MARCUS AURELIUS

Human nature makes it easy for us to blame our misfortune on a single issue or person.

Doing this can blind us from reality and sets us up for additional problems.

I've learned that in most instances, whatever is troubling me is the nexus of a number of factors, not the least of which are often my previous decisions, comments and actions.

Whenever I'm tempted to point the finger of blame at others, I try to pause and ask myself if I need to point it at myself, too.

In most instances, I realize that in some way I added to or even caused the problem.

Personal Accountability > Blaming Others

"How does it help . . . to make troubles heavier by bemoaning them?"

—SENECA

I t's human nature to feel sorry for ourselves whenever we are faced with problems.

While it does feel good to vent and "blow off steam" when faced with a difficult situation, experience has taught me that this does nothing to bring forth a resolution, and often makes things worse.

Actions to Solve Problems > Whining About Problems

"Smart people learn from everything and everyone, average people from their experiences, stupid people already have the answers."

—SOCRATES

There's no doubt that I have exhibited all of these traits during my life.

Lessons learned while being smart have been the best and easiest to implement.

Being average has caused me more trouble than I'd like to admit, because the lessons were often learned via some very painful experiences.

In almost every instance where I believed that I had all of the answers, I inevitably learned that I didn't know what I didn't know, and that allowing myself to approach situations in this manner was the height of stupidity and never resulted in a positive outcome.

Smart people take deliberate steps to avoid being average, and they recognize that arrogance and overconfidence can cause them to act stupidly!

"Dripping water hollows out stone, not through force but through persistence."

—OVID

xperience has taught me that the best things in life rarely come easily or quickly.

I've often failed or achieved dismal results when first pursuing them.

In most instances, the key to eventually success was my willingness to get up, dust myself off and try again, even when facing great disappointment, embarrassment, or criticism.

I've learned that achieving lofty goals is actually quite simple:

Never Stop Trying!

"Our greatest effort should be to show how firmly we retain the memory of the favors we have received. This requires constant renewal, since no one can repay a favor unless he remembers the favor."

—SENECA

Any success that I have achieved was made possible by countless people who supported me in various ways. They were often "in the shadows" where others could not see what they were doing to help me.

Over time, I learned to reach out to these "invisible people" and make sure they knew that I was aware of their efforts, and how much I appreciated them.

I urge you to reflect upon the people who have helped you, or are helping you in some way, and resolve to tell them how much you value them.

It's never too late to show someone how grateful you are to have them in your life.

Do this now, while you still can; don't put it off until tomorrow.

Because our tomorrows are not guaranteed.

"How many have laid waste to your life when you weren't aware of what you were losing, how much was wasted in pointless grief, foolish joy, greedy desire, and social amusements—how little of your own was left to you. You will realize you are dying before your time!"

—SENECA

Associating with certain individuals can cause us to drift from the course we have set for our lives.

This drift can be visible or subtle, but in either case, we can suddenly find ourselves in situations that we'd have never imagined we'd be in.

One of the most important choices we face is who we allow to be in our lives.

All choices have consequences, and this is one that deserves our best thinking.

"Take a good hard look at people's ruling principle, especially of the wise, what they run away from and what they seek out."

—MARCUS AURELIUS

Initial impressions projected by certain individuals are often inaccurate, and they are sometimes quite deceptive.

I've learned to evaluate people less by what they say, and more by what they do or don't do.

An individual's sound character will surface by their actions when faced with adversity, stress, and situations that clash with their self-interests.

If they lack sound character, this too, will become apparent after some time, as you see them respond to various situations with a lack of integrity, or selfishness, or mean-spirited behavior.

I'm quite capable of being overly impressed by someone's past successes and reputation. One of the biggest lessons I've learned is to allow a good amount of time to pass before I finalize my judgement of this person's character and moral compass.

"Keep constant guard over your perceptions, for it is no small thing you are protecting, but your respect, trustworthiness and steadiness, peace of mind, freedom from pain and fear, in a word your freedom. For what would you sell these things?"

—EPICTETUS

The situations and environments we choose for ourselves (or tolerate being subjected to) are the main drivers of our thoughts.

I've learned to continuously evaluate the situations, environments, and relationships associated with my life so I can identify sources of unnecessary stress, friction, disappointment, and unhappiness.

Once identified, I eliminate those that I'm able to, and minimize my exposure to those I cannot.

Asking myself these questions (and being honest as I answer them) makes this process quite easier:

- Why am I doing this?
- Why am I tolerating this?
- Is this helping or harming the achievement of my goals?
- Does this add to or detract from my happiness?
- Do I have the ability to distance myself from this?
- What can I do right now to make my life better?

Some of these questions yield answers that present difficult choices, and experience has taught me that it's almost always better to make difficult choices earlier rather than later.

"It is quite impossible to unite happiness with a yearning for what we don't have. Happiness has all that it wants, and resembling the well-fed, there shouldn't be hunger or thirst."

—Epictetus

I'm a goal-oriented "self-starter" type of person. I am always striving to do more, achieve more, and learn more.

For much of my life, the pursuit of new and exciting goals resulted in me being so focused and driven that I often lost sight of the successes I'd already achieved.

Eventually, I realized that my continuous quest for self-improvement was preventing me from pausing and reflecting upon the fact that I had accomplished most of the things that I'd set out to do, and that I should allow myself to feel happiness and a sense of satisfaction from a job well done.

I've learned that the excitement associated with facing challenging goals becomes even greater after reflecting on goals already achieved, especially those I once viewed daunting and perhaps even unattainable.

> *"So, concerning the things we pursue, and for which we vigorously exert ourselves, we owe this consideration—either there is nothing useful in them, or most aren't useful. Some of them are superfluous, while others aren't worth that much. But we don't discern this and see them as free, when they cost us dearly."*
>
> **—SENECA**

My desires and ambitions changed greatly as I matured and reflected upon the lessons that life was teaching me.

Often, I was unaware of these lessons, and the longer I remained oblivious to them, the more disappointment or stress I felt, and the greater the precious time wasted.

Over time, I realized that while my character, integrity, moral compass, and sense of honor were rightfully "carved in stone" and had never changed, many of the things I had deemed essential to my success and happiness were far more image than substance.

Things I once considered of the greatest importance later seemed trivial due to the added perspective provided by a few more years of life experience.

I now realize that the ability to remain focused on that which really matters in this life is the key to true happiness.

*"No sooner said than done—so acts
your man of worth."*

—QUINTUS ENNIUS

The world is full of honorable people who have excellent ideas, but for some reason, they often fail to take actions required to execute and bring them to fruition.

By observing others who'd achieved things I aspired to, I've learned that most worthy accomplishments begin inside a person's mind; the mental battle that pits the desire for success and satisfaction against ego, pride, and fear of failure or embarrassment.

One way I've learned to win this mental battle is to force myself to "Start Ugly" and simply begin the attack on the desired goal, vice putting it off until a beautifully elegant plan can be created.

For me, "Starting Ugly" has often proven to be the wellspring of the accomplishments and accolades that I am most proud of.

*Average Idea Acted Upon Now > Excellent Idea Hostage
to Perpetual Planning*

> *"Do not forget, a man needs little to lead a happy life."*
>
> —MARCUS AURELIUS

As a young man observing people who appeared to be successful and happy, I associated their happiness with the possession of material things. I thought they were happy because they'd been able to acquire the trappings of successful, lavish lifestyles.

So, not knowing better, I thought that I would also be happier if I was able to do the same.

I was wrong about many of them, and about myself.

Suffice it to say that I know more than a few "Miserable Millionaires," who despite vast wealth and material possessions, lead very unfulfilled and unhappy lives.

Conversely, I know many people of modest means who are among the happiest people I've ever known. They almost always radiate self-confidence and a zest for life.

Personally, I've learned that my happiness depends little on the possessions I can acquire, and almost entirely on people I love and appreciate, and seek only the same from them in return.

"*Everywhere chance reigns, just cast out your line and where you least expect it, there waits a fish in the swirling waters.*"

—OVID

L ooking back, some of the best opportunities ever presented to me came from people and situations that I hadn't initially viewed in a positive manner.

On more than one occasion, I agreed to do something because I felt that I had to, not because I wanted to.

Often, these situations were not the unpleasant experiences that I'd anticipated they'd be, they actually turned out to be incredibly rewarding and impactful on my life's direction.

What I learned was that if I approached all relationships, situations, and tasks with a resolve to do my best with a cheerful "Can Do" attitude, my life was enriched by the experience more often than not.

"When evil times prevail, take care to preserve the serenity of your heart."

—HORACE

I think it is common for people going through tough situations to become dejected or even angry to the point that they begin to view everything in a negative manner.

At times, I've allowed myself to project the negativity, disappointment, or hurt from one situation or relationship onto other aspects of my life that were actually going quite well.

I've learned that when tough times come, it's wise to take time to reflect on all of the good things and people in my life. Doing so helps me quickly transition from "Woe is me" to "I've got this!"

Life will bring forth tough times, but they cannot conquer a focused, determined mind that is fueled by a heart that is calm, self-assured, and full of happiness.

"From this instant on, vow to stop disappointing yourself. Separate yourself from the mob. Decide to be extraordinary and do what you need to do—now."

—EPICTETUS

A disturbing trend in recent times is the celebration of victimhood, even when those with the sad stories are victims of their own doing.

In almost every instance, my life's failures and disappointments were the direct result of my decisions, actions and inactions.

Just by admitting this, I begin to separate myself from those who would encourage me to place the blame elsewhere, and this is a "mob" that is best left behind sooner vice later.

This world is full of winners and whiners.

I want to be a winner and perhaps even an extraordinary man.

The choice is mine to make, and the work required is mine to do.

*"To live a good life: We have the potential for it.
If we can learn to be indifferent to
what makes no difference."*

—MARCUS AURELIUS

A powerful statement from this Roman Emperor.
While it is good to have mentors and seek advice and direction, I alone am responsible for defining what a "Good Life" looks like for me.

My definition has changed greatly over the years, as I matured and learned what was truly important to my happiness.

A huge part of this was learning to recognize whether the people or things in my life were more image than substance.

I've learned to try to focus on seeking substance in all aspects of my life, and that to do so often requires patience and close scrutiny, lest I be fooled or unduly influenced by "false advertising."

"Above all, keep a close watch on this—that you are never so tied to your former acquaintances and friends that you are pulled down to their level. If you don't, you'll be ruined. . . . You must choose whether to be loved by these friends and remain the same person, or to become a better person at the cost of those friends . . . if you try to have it both ways you will neither make progress nor keep what you once had."

—Epictetus

It's a fact that people change during their lives relative to their values, attitudes, goals and behaviors.

What was once a healthy and mutually beneficial friendship or relationship can become stagnant at best, and negative or even destructive at worst.

Remembering that people almost always become like those they associate with, it is critical to remain vigilant and ask the tough, but necessary question:

"Am I better off by allowing this person to be in my life?"

So often, we cling to friendships and relationships out of a sense of loyalty, despite knowing that they are not good for us and haven't been for quite some time.

It takes moral courage to insist on having an inner circle that is worthy of you, and vice-versa.

That said, I don't believe that anyone can truly reach the heights of their potential without being willing to repeatedly exhibit moral courage.

The "tree" of one's inner circle must be carefully attended to, and pruned on occasion, to enable it to remain healthy and bear fruit over many seasons.

*"Throw out your conceited opinions,
for it is impossible for a person to begin to
learn what he thinks he already knows."*

—EPICTETUS

As a young man desiring to be respected and held in high regard by my associates, I assumed the best way to achieve this was to appear knowledgeable, competent, and in full command of all topics and situations.

Obviously, this is not possible for anyone to do, especially a young man who was too inexperienced and overconfident to even consider the possibility that he "didn't know what he didn't know!"

After learning too many lessons the hard way, I realized that my approach was not working well and that I needed to seek the knowledge, insights, and guidance of those more experienced than me.

My successes and the associated respect and high regard from others increased exponentially once I learned to stop talking and start listening.

Any person that does this, while surrounding themselves with people smarter and more experienced than they are, will be capable of achieving superior results in all aspects of life.

> *"Well-being is realized by small steps,*
> *but is truly no small thing."*
>
> **—ZENO**

As a young athlete and early on in my service as a US Marine, I assumed that my well-being related almost entirely to my physical conditioning.

I was too inexperienced to fully understand the importance of being in a state of harmony mentally, physically, and spiritually, and that a proper balance among them was one of the "secrets to success."

As I matured, I realized that I performed best in every aspect of my life when I consciously worked on maintaining a good balance amongst them, and that whenever I allowed myself to focus too much on one at the expense of the others, my performance suffered.

I learned through personal experience and the observation of people I admired that one's quest for excellence must always be fueled by placing a premium on a continuous investment in one's well-being.

"If you find something very difficult to achieve yourself, don't imagine it impossible—for anything possible and proper for another person can be achieved as easily by you."

—MARCUS AURELIUS

My personal and professional growth was maximized and accelerated by attempting things that I was unsure that I could achieve, or that others told me that I was not capable of doing.

In some instances, the thought of trying to do these things intimidated me; occasionally, they even frightened me.

Over time, I realized that by assessing a challenge logically, and observing what others had done to successfully conquer it, there was no reason why I couldn't conquer it, too.

Ultimately, I came to believe that there was almost nothing I couldn't accomplish if I was willing to commit to "putting in the work."

My advice to others who have big dreams and lofty goals is to ask themselves, "Why not me, and why not now?"

And then . . . take action!

*"Just as one person delights in improving his
farm, and another his horse, so I delight in
attending to my own improvement day by day."*

—SOCRATES

If I've learned anything during my life it is this:

Most highly successful people never stop trying to improve themselves mentally, physically and spiritually.

In almost every instance in which I've observed or studied high achievers, they continue to remain "students of the game" long after they've reached noteworthy levels of success.

Experience and maturity have enabled me to arrive at a point in my life where I take the time to enjoy and be proud of the successes I've been fortunate to have, while knowing that these successes are often fleeting and can be lost if they are not continuously attended to and improved upon.

*"The price of apathy towards public affairs is to
be ruled by evil men."*

—PLATO

Regarding politics and those who manage to be elected to high office, Plato's ancient words are entirely relevant today.

Most Americans are uninformed, unaware or uncaring about the true character and motives of their elected officials. Their apathy or blind loyalty to a political party or ideology allows our country to be influenced and harmed by unsavory individuals who care little about the welfare of the nation and its citizens, and more about their own personal gain.

This will not end well for America.

Likewise, apathy toward those we allow to be in our lives on a personal and professional level almost always leads to similarly poor results, along with broken hearts and unfulfilled hopes and dreams.

Apathy is a poison that resides in the minds of people who have surrendered to mediocrity.

"We don't abandon our pursuits because we despair of ever perfecting them."

—EPICTETUS

As a young man, I sometimes became discouraged when realizing that a goal I'd set for myself was turning out to be very difficult to accomplish, and perhaps even impossible.

A couple of times, I stopped pursuing a goal because of this, only to reconsider my approach years later and realize success.

This taught me to expect friction, setbacks and disappointment whenever I was seeking to achieve difficult things, and that it was during these moments when force of will and rational thinking were essential.

And most of all, I began to understand that most of the value in striving to achieve difficult things is not gained from their achievement, but from the journey itself.

"Many words have been spoken by Plato, Zeno, Chrysippus, Posidonius, and by a whole host of equally excellent Stoics. I'll tell you how people can prove their words to be their own—by putting into practice what they've been preaching."

—SENECA

As a lifelong learner and follower of ancient philosophers, I have always been impressed by their wisdom.

In many ways, they all ascribe to the same core principles and philosophies, even though some of them lived centuries apart, or came from different civilizations and nation-states.

Seneca's simple advice remains relevant to anyone desiring to learn from the hard-won lessons of the past: Replicate the wisdom and sound behavior of others . . . every single day!

I've learned that the best course of action for any person who aspires to live an honorable, happy, and productive life, is to simply determine what kind of man or woman they want to be known as and ensure that their every decision and action in some way supports and enables this vision.

"It is essential for you to remember that the attention you give to any action should be in due proportion to its worth, for then you won't tire and give up, if you aren't busying yourself with lesser things beyond what should be allowed."

—MARCUS AURELIUS

Time is a precious and irreplaceable resource, and like most people, I've wasted or misused more of it during my life than I like to admit.

I've learned through personal experience and by observing others that one of the surest ways to squander one's time is to use it on relatively insignificant matters at the expense of those that are far more important.

Whether acting as in individual, teammate, leader, parent, or friend, one must constantly assess how this precious resource is being expended, and to ensure that it is being applied to matters of the highest urgency and with the greatest potential return on time invested.

"Success comes to the lowly and to the poorly talented, but the special characteristic of a great person is to triumph over the disasters and panics of human life."

—SENECA

It's true that success is not limited solely to those who work hard. Some people just seem to have a knack for being in the right place at the right time, and they often reap benefits well out of proportion to the amount of work they did.

I do not begrudge these people their seemingly "unearned successes." The truth is that while I have worked very hard to achieve certain things, I have also had the good luck to be in the right place at the right time several times in my life.

I have learned to happily accept good luck whenever it comes to me, but to never expect it to be the solution to any of my problems, or to hand me easy victories over difficult situations.

"How much better to heal than seek revenge from injury. Vengeance wastes a lot of time and exposes you to many more injuries than the first that sparked it. Anger always outlasts hurt. Best to take the opposite course. Would anyone think it normal to return a kick to a mule or a bite to a dog?"

—SENECA

Profound comments from this wise Stoic.

I wish I'd learned this lesson much earlier in my life: "Anger always outlasts hurt."

My natural personality is to be happy and friendly to others. I tend to give people the benefit of the doubt and allow their behavior to help me finalize my opinions of them.

That said, as a "born scrapper," I was never one to run from a fight or any form of insult (real or perceived). As a younger man, my "default setting" was to respond in kind or to seek vengeance in some way.

Now, in some instances, that type of reaction was entirely justified. But, with the benefit of added maturity, I look back at some of the things that I became angry over, and I wonder why I allowed myself to waste such time and energy?

Once I realized that remaining angry at a person or situation never made things better for me (and often made things worse!), I understood that the best response to anything that angered me was to "let it go" mentally and resume thoughts and actions that made my life better and happier.

Be wary of anger, as it can damage your mental and physical health as badly as the sustained abuse of alcohol, illicit drugs or other forms of destructive behavior!

> *"Each person acquires their own character, but their official roles are designated by chance. You should invite some to your table because they are deserving, others because they may come to deserve it."*
>
> **—SENECA**

I have always tried to surround myself with exceptional people, especially those I can learn from.

At every stage of my life, various high achievers invited me to their table not because I was deserving, but because they saw something in me that caused them to believe that I might one day not only deserve to sit with them, but to add value to the discussion.

It was this steady stream of "helping hands" that helped me experience significant growth in all aspects of my life, and I am grateful for their patience and generosity.

I am happy to say that even now, at the age of 65, I am still being invited to sit at tables that I am not deserving of in any way, mostly because I have earned a reputation for behaving as a good student should.

Having benefitted from so many extraordinary teachers, leaders, mentors and friends, I feel an obligation to invite lesser experienced and developed people into my inner circle, so I can share with them the many lessons I learned from others much smarter, wiser, and far more accomplished than I am.

At this point in my life, the only thing I value more than the wisdom and knowledge I've managed to acquire, is the act of sharing it with others!

"Don't allow yourself to be heard any longer griping about public life, not even with your own ears!"

—MARCUS AURELIUS

As a Marine Corps leader, I compiled a list of 24 quotes and statements that captured my philosophy of leadership and overall approach to being a Marine. I referred to this document as "Ettore's Rules."

This is Rule #20:

"Know the difference between pain and discomfort. Don't snivel . . . ever."

The implied message to all Marines within my unit was this: "We all volunteered to be Marines, and Marines often have to do difficult things in extremely challenging and dangerous environments. There will be discomfort and perhaps even pain, but there will be no tolerance for whining, especially among those in leadership positions."

This sentiment is relevant to most of the various phases of our lives; when we are students, athletes, teammates, coaches, leaders, spouses, parents and friends.

Each of these phases are often associated with challenging situations that require one to make difficult decisions, and experience has taught me that positive outcomes come only when I focus on effecting solutions to my problems vice complaining or whining about them.

Among Marines, there is a general disdain and lack of respect for those prone to snivel.

I've found this to be true in all other environments I've operated in.

Simply put, life's winners are never whiners!

"Your principles can't be extinguished unless you snuff out the thoughts that feed them, for it's continually in your power to reignite new ones. . . . It's possible to start living again! See things anew as you once did— that is how to restart life!"

—MARCUS AURELIUS

Like most people, I have experienced both good and bad times during my life.

Many of the accomplishments that I am most proud of resulted from personal growth experienced while navigating what often seemed to be insurmountable problems and situations.

With the benefit of hindsight applied to the 65 years I've been alive, it is clear to me that even though the difficult periods of my life were typically not a good place to be, they were almost always a great place to be from!

"From Rusticus . . . I learned to read carefully and not be satisfied with a rough understanding of the whole, and not to agree too quickly with those who have a lot to say about something."

—MARCUS AURELIUS

As a young man, my parents, teachers, coaches and mentors advised me to be skeptical of things that seemed "too good to be true."

And, like many young men, I didn't heed their counsel to the extent that I should have at times, and I learned some tough lessons finding out what they knew to be true:

"If it seems too good to be true, it probably is!"

One of the most important lessons I learned in this regard was to control my emotions and remain objective when facing something that not only seemed to be true, but that I really wanted to be true because of how it could benefit me in some way.

One of my flaws is that I tend to see only the good in people I meet, even if it isn't there.

I've learned that evaluating people less on what they say and more on what they actually do, is something that requires constant vigilance.

Recommended Reading

There are hundreds of books on Stoicism available, some written by the ancient philosophers or their followers, and others by more contemporary authors. Each book I have read on the subject has contributed to my understanding of Stoic philosophy and how I can incorporate its teachings into my personal and professional lives.

Shown below is a brief list of books that I feel can help individuals quickly enhance their understanding of Stoicism. These books do not have to be read in the order shown below, and my experience has been that it can be quite enlightening to read one of the ancient classics at the same time as one written in recent times. For me, the back and forth between ancient times and the present was very helpful in enhancing my ability to integrate the wisdom and insights of the Wise Old Men into my life.

Classic Books on Stoicism

Meditations by Marcus Aurelius

This could easily pass as one of the most profound writings on stoicism. I'd say this is the Stoic Bible. It was enlightening, and the writing style presented an in-depth touch on the core and fundamental values of stoic philosophy.

Meditations is a unique document and probably the only one of its kind in written form. It is a detailed account of the thoughts and meditations of Marcus Aurelius, who was one of the most extraordinary Roman emperors. The book was written in a style that was both reflective and honest. It contains advice from the emperor to himself on ways to have and make better judgments, make good on the responsibilities and obligations demanded of his position. From the book, we'll see how a man still strived to remain humble and empathetic despite his status and power. Marcus always took time every night to practice some spiritual exercise which helped to remind him of the need to remain patient, humble, generous, and empathetic irrespective of the situation or status he found himself in.

I'd strongly recommend this book as it is an embodiment of very practical philosophies.

Letters of a Stoic by Seneca

Seneca served as a moral guide for others, and this book provides bits of advice and counsel he shared with his followers.

I enjoyed reading this book; there was a lot to learn from it. His advice on grief, power, wealth, religion, and life, in general, was excellent and full of moral principles to live by. You'd also find his short essays on the brevity of life worthy of your time.

Discourses by Epictetus

Epictetus was a Roman slave who was able to earn his freedom and went on to became a very effective teacher and philosopher. His teachings were able to survive, all thanks to his student named Arrian. Arrian is credited with transcribing the lessons and lectures of Epictetus' classroom in the second century AD. Arrian was noted to have written in a letter before the publication of the Discourses "whatever I used to hear him say I write down, word for word, as best as I could, as a record for later use of his thought and frank expression."

Later on, Arrian used these notes to gain a reputation in Rome and served as a political advisor, military commander, and later went on to write books of his own.

Marcus Aurelius expressed gratitude to his philosophy teacher Rusticus in his first book of Meditations, titled "Debts and Lessons." He thanked him for introducing him to the teachings of Epictetus and loaning him a copy of the book.

The Letters of Seneca to Lucilius

Reading Seneca is always a delight. The way he brings meaning and insight to even the fundamental aspect of life is just fantastic. Seneca wrote in Latin, whereas Aurelius and Epictetus, although Romans, wrote in Greek. Although Seneca's time preceded theirs, there was never a mention of his name in their books or writing.

Seneca had quite a different approach to stoicism. His letters to Lucilius go with other names, but they all make up the bulk of the collection referred to as Moral Letters written by Seneca. The letters are well-written essays that contain wisdom, guidance, basic life knowledge, and teachings addressed to a novice stoic.

The Writings of Cicero

Although Cicero wasn't a Stoic but a Platonist, he still wrote on many ideas from which we have drawn what we may today refer to as our primary sources of information on stoicism. Cicero, like Seneca, wrote in Latin. Cicero was a very learned man who had gone to Athens to study and had a profound knowledge of stoic teachings and principles.

Cicero has so many writings on stoicism, and most notable is his De Finibus ("On Moral Ends"), a book made up of a series of dialogues. It was a fascinating collection; here, Cicero created a world of philosophers from different schools of thought. Philosophers who represented Epicureanism, Stoicism, and Platonism, and they took turns criticizing other's philosophies and providing details and descriptions of their religion.

The book draws upon early Greek stoic ideas and teachings and gives a detailed and much better account of stoic ethics in a somewhat systematic way; here, you'll find a more robust discussion of Stoic ethics that cannot be found in the works or writings of Seneca or Marcus Aurelius.

Lectures and Fragments by Musonius Rufus

Gaius Musonius Rufius was popularly referred to as the Roman Socrates, and his philosophies, principles and ideas are expressed in this book.. There is no account of him writing about himself, and most of what he wrote didn't even survive over time. However, the teachings found in this book were formed from the 32 apothegms and 21 discourses written down and discussed by his students.

Musonius was a practical philosopher and frowned at theories. He taught using very practical arguments and discussions that were designed to incentivize others to take positive actions immediately. He firmly believed that philosophy is the practice of virtues and good behaviors. He wasn't interested in luxury, and some of his teachings even condemned it.

Epictetus, a student of Musonius, mentioned his name several times in his famous Discourses.

Contemporary Books on Stoicism

How to think like a Roman Emperor by Donald Robertson
This book is exciting in that it presents the life and philosophy of Marcus Aurelius in an exciting and modern way. Donald is a well-known figure of Modern Stoicism and also a cognitive psychotherapist. This book will provide a modern-day guide to stoic wisdom.

Stoicism and the Art of Happiness by Donald Robertson.
The book demystifies various misconceptions about stoicism and shows what stoicism stands for in modern times. This book provides different exercises and activities that anyone can try while taking their first steps into the stoic way of life. The author emphasizes the need to build character and virtue other than pursuing pleasure and excitement.

The Obstacle is the Way by Ryan Holiday
Marcus Aurelius said, "The impediment to action advances action. What stands in the way becomes the way". This maxim was what inspired this amazing book by Ryan Holiday where he explores the whole idea of resistance while trying to build better habits and behaviors. The book is significant because it teaches how to thrive under pressure and provides fundamental principles that guide living with the demands and stress of daily life.

Ryan Holiday achieved this using historical examples of great men and women; it teaches us how to accept and love our fate and not be bothered by the consequences or things that come with it. The book also teaches overcoming adversity and difficulties and finding our way through every obstacle or opposition.

Over time, the book has received a massive readership, with coaches and athletes alike feasting on its wealth of knowledge and gaining some meaning for their lives. It has also been featured in prominent magazines such as Sports Illustrated and ESPN.

The Daily Stoic by **Ryan Holiday and Stephen Hanselman**

The Daily Stoic: 366 Meditations on Wisdom, Perseverance and the Art of Living contains stoic passages containing very exciting stories and explanations of the stoic principles proposed by Stoic "heavyweights" such as Marcus Aurelius, Seneca, and Epictetus, and lesser-known philosophers such as Chrysippus, Cleanthes, and Zeno.

This book is designed to be read like a devotional: one passage or chapter per day that causes the reader to reflect upon his or her understanding of character, virtue, and morals and how they can find ways to apply newly found insights and ideas in their daily lives.

How to Be a Stoic: *Ancient Wisdom for Modern Living* by **Massimo Pigliucci**

This book talks about the relationship between stoicism and modern-day living. It talks about the relationship between stoicism and scientific worldviews and how it can coexist with atheism and agnosticism. Massimo, a career philosopher, provides helpful, practical guides of stoic wisdom for everyday living.

Guide To the Good Life: *The Ancient Art of Stoic Joy* by **William Irvine**

Irvine explores how the teachings and ideas of Stoic philosophy are still relevant in this time and age. He provides a refreshing way of seeing stoicism and how the ancient philosophy can still direct lives and produce better individuals with better moral standards. In this book, Irvine provides a road map for anyone just getting into the stoic way of life and philosophy.

The Handbook for New Stoics: *How to Thrive in a World Out of Your Control – 52 week-by-week Lessons* by **Massimo Pigliucci, Gregory Lopez.**

This book was written by world-renowned stoic practitioners Massimo Pigliucci and Gregory Lopez. It provides a series of weekly lessons for beginners and covers an entire year. It touches several aspects of stoic philosophy on topics such as desire, patience, courage, and temperance and how to apply this ageless wisdom in our modern way of living.

In conclusion, these and other books can form the foundation of a complete and self-taught education on the philosophy of Stoicism.

Conclusion

In conclusion, Stoicism provides wisdom, insights, and guidance that can help us navigate the inevitable rocks and shoals of life. Stoics are not scared of death; rather, they understand that death is our destiny and, as such, we should focus on living our lives to the fullest extent possible and seize each day with vigor and enthusiasm.

Stoicism teaches us to be humble, to focus our energy on the things we can control, to face problems with strength, to have the confidence to ask for help when necessary, to be a life-long learner, continuously striving to gain understanding. In short, the stoics teach us to pursue self-improvement in all aspects and at all times in order to live better lives and bring improvement to all that we touch. When we know better, we can do better!

Acknowledgements

I was blessed to have served with exceptional leaders and role models throughout my two decades of service as a U.S. Marine. Many of these warriors had fought in savage battles in the Pacific during World War II, in the bitter cold hills and mountains of Korea and in the unforgiving jungles of Vietnam. Their experiences left all of them them indelibly changed for the rest of their lives, and with the benefit of hindsight and increased awareness of the price many warriors pay for serving in combat, I now know that many of them were dealing with what is commonly referred to as Post-Traumatic Stress Disorder. However, the vast majority of them were not only able to cope effectively with the psychological scars that were produced by their prolonged exposure to the battlefield, they were able to learn how to cope with their issues and overcome them.

Observing how these Marines, many of them combat veterans of the three afore mentioned wars, went about their daily lives and carried out their duties inspired me during my early days as a young enlisted Marine. Simply put, I admired these men, perhaps even to the point of idolizing them, and I spent my entire career in the Marine Corps trying to live up to their combat legacy and leadership by example.

I learned so much from interacting with and observing them, and I quickly realized that they all valued education and the life-long pursuit of knowledge, and that they placed great value on the lessons of the past, especially those associated with warfare, so that the failures and successes of past combat leaders could be leveraged appropriately. It was through their example that I became a lifelong learner and student of history and anything else that could help me become a better Marine and combat leader, and it was through some of them that I became aware of the philosophy known as Stoicism. Of the many "gifts" these stalwart Marine leaders gave me, this one, the exposure to the timeless wisdom of the ancient Stoic philosophers, was clearly one that had a profound and life-long impact upon me, and for this and all of what these men did for me, I am eternally grateful.

I'm also thankful for the patient support of my fellow Marine and close friend, Nancy Broding, for all that she did to help me take this book from my initial vision to completion and publica-tions. Few people know me better on a personal level than does Nancy, and this enables her to read and edit my writing quite effec-tively. Simply put, if Nancy suggests a change in something I've written, I do it without hesitation! Thank you, Nancy, for not only being a great editor, but for being one of my closest friends and one that I've repeatedly turned to for help during some of the most challenging periods of my life.

Elena Reznikova merits special recognition for her patience and unequaled skill as the creator of the covers, graphics and the formatting for all of my books. I'm fortunate to know her!

Gratitude

To Wendy,

My dear friend and trusted confidant . . . a beacon of hope during some of my life's most difficult times . . . sharer of Rolex moments . . . patient, kind and loving . . . always looking out for my best interests. You have a special place in my heart forever!

"She helped me find the courage to confront
my fears and cut through excuses."

Also by Mike Ettore

TRUST-BASED LEADERSHIP™:
Marine Corps Leadership Concepts
For Today's Business Leaders

by Mike Ettore

ISBNs:
Paperback: 978-0-9898229-4-7
Hardcover: 978-0-9898229-8-5
Ebook: 978-0-9898229-5-4

Available at:
Amazon, Barnes&Noble.com, Kindle, iBooks, and many other retailers

This 574 page book details how the author effectively adapted and applied
Marine Corps leadership concepts while serving as a business leader—
and how he leverages the Trust-Based Leadership™ model to help others
become World-Class Leaders.

Section I – Marine Corps Leadership
Section II – Trust-Based Leadership™
Section III – The Trust-Based Leader
Section IV – Lessons Learned
Section V – Leadership Articles

Mike is highly regarded for his unique ability to help leaders rapidly elevate
their skills as they create and sustain high-performance teams. He wrote this
book to help leaders at all levels maximize their potential and become World
Class Leaders.

Also by Mike Ettore

PRINCIPLES OF WAR
FOR THE CORPORATE BATTLEFIELD:
Warfighting Lessons for Business Leaders

by Mike Ettore

Isbns:
Paperback: 978-0-9898229-9-2
Hardcover: 978-1-7372881-0-7
Ebook: 978-1-7372881-1-4

Available at:
Amazon, Barnes&Noble.com, Kindle, iBooks, and many other retailers

The "missions" of the business battlefield are not dissimilar from actual military battlefields . . . establishing the desired end state, describing and assigning the necessary tasks, designing and task-organizing the unit to best support mission accomplishment, assembling and developing the team, and achieving operational unity of effort via timely and precise communications.

The risks associated with both battlefields are similar as well. It is almost inevitable that soldiers may die or become wounded in combat and their units may suffer loss. Likewise, a company may fail and place the livelihoods and welfare its employees at great risk. While this does not bring forth the physical risks associated with war, business failures are personally damaging and the negative effects are lasting.

This book contains examples of how each principle has been successfully applied in both military and business environments, and it **will enable business leaders to quickly and effectively apply The Principles of War in their own planning and operations.**

The graphics used in *Principles of War for the Corporate Battlefield* and *Trust-Based Leadership*™ and additional resources are available for free in the Bonus Resource Vault, which you can find at:

HTTPS://FIDELISLEADERSHIP.COM/BOOKBONUS

Social Media – Let's Stay In Touch!

Fidelis Leadership Podcast: https://www.fidelisleadership.com/podcast

Facebook
- Fidelis: www.facebook.com/FidelisLeadershipGroup
- Mike: www.facebook.com/EttoreMike

Linkedin:
- Fidelis: www.linkedin.com/company/fidelis-leadership-group-llc
- Mike: www.linkedin.com/in/mikeettore/

Twitter: https://twitter.com/FidelisLeader

Instagram: www.instagram.com/fidelisleadership/

Fidelis Leadership Newsletter

Receive monthly emails containing valuable lessons, tactics and techniques that can help you become a World-Class Leader! I promise that I will never share your contact information in any way, and if you decide to stop receiving the newsletter you can unsubscribe with one click.

SIGN UP NOW! HTTPS://FIDELISLEADERSHIP.COM

"A PLACE OF LEARNING FOR THOSE ASPIRING TO LEADERSHIP EXCELLENCE!"

The Fidelis Leadership Podcast is for those who want to become World Class Leaders. Weekly episodes convey lessons and advice from some of the world's foremost leadership experts, and discussions regarding the effective application of the Trust-Based Leadership™ model.

HTTPS://WWW.FIDELISLEADERSHIP.COM/PODCAST

Also Found on Your Favorite Podcast Platforms!

From the Author

Book Reviews

Thank you for reading my book. Please consider visiting the site where you purchased it and writing a brief review. Your feedback is important to me and will help others decide whether to read the book too.

New Books, Training Programs and Events

If you'd like to get notifications of my latest books, training programs and leadership events, please join my email list by visiting https://fidelisleadership.com

Bulk Purchase Discounts

If you would like to purchase 25 or more print copies of this book, we are happy to offer you a discount on the net list price of the book. Please send inquiries to: info@fidelisleadership.com

Fidelis Leadership Group
— Developing World Class Leaders —

My Services

Executive Coaching

My executive coaching engagements are uniquely tailored to each individual and are designed to provide focus that can deepen an executive's self-awareness and promote personal and professional growth. The private coaching sessions provide leaders with an opportunity to engage in focused, constructive, and confidential dialogue with a skilled and objective listener. I collaborate with each leader to design a program that fosters and accelerates individual growth, while providing the coaching and facilitation to achieve desired outcomes.

Leadership Development

I help educate, train, and coach leaders so they can dramatically accelerate their personal and professional development. I work best with clients who operate in a culture of execution, accountability, and leadership by example—or those who desire to create such a culture within their organizations. I offer customized leadership training and development programs—including onsite training seminars - for leaders at every level: C-Suite and SVP-VP-Director level, high-potential individuals and others serving in mid-level and front-line leadership roles.

Speaking

I am an experienced public speaker with a strong history of delivering dynamic, interactive, and memorable presentations and keynote speeches to a wide range of organizations. Leveraging leadership lessons that were forged in the unforgiving crucible of combat and while serving as a senior executive, I inspire and energize my audiences and provide them with actionable strategies, tactics, and techniques that they can implement immediately upon returning to their teams.

CONTACT ME NOW!
info@fidelisleadership.com